ENVIRONMENT AND HUMAN RIGHTS

ENVIRONMENT AND HUMAN RIGHTS

Dr. Mohd. Yousuf Bhat
M.A., Ph.D. (Human Rights)

Reference Press
Delhi

First Published 2004

ISBN : 81-88583-68-5

Price : Rs. 475/-

Published by :

Reference Press

4831/24, Ansari Road, Darya Ganj,
New Delhi - 110 002
Phone : 23260807
Fax : 23274173
E-mail: info@essessreference.com
url:http://www.essessreference.com

Printed at :

Mehra Offset Press, New Delhi.

Dedicated to my

DEAREST PARENTS

and

Dearest Sister

(LATE) SHAMIMA AKHTAR

Contents

Preface

Everyone likes to live in a healthy environment which is a basic human necessity. Healthy environment is a nature's gift. Air, water, and land are essential for all living beings. Any discharge of material or energy into water, air or land that causes acute (short term) or chronic (long term) detriment to the earth's ecological balance and lowers the quality of life is known as pollution. In legal literature pollution has been described as a deliberate or accidental contamination of environment with man's wastes or as a matter in the wrong place at wrong time and in wrong quantity or anything released into environment which impairs or degrades it.

The industrialisation of society, the introduction of motorized vehicles, and the explosion of human population, have caused an exponential growth in the production of goods and services. In line with this growth there has been a tremendous increase in waste by-products. The indiscriminate discharge of untreated industrial wastes containing most insidious and persistent toxic pollutants into waterways, the spewing of thousands of tons of particulate and air-borne gases into atmosphere, indiscriminate use of plastic bags, the 'throwaway' attitude towards solid wastes, in brief man's instinct of selfishness, profit-oriented motto led him towards indiscriminate exploitation of natural wealth. In this way, it imbalances the nature's capacity of self-stabilization.

We, humans are, as Virgina W. Rasmussen puts it, 'technological creatures' and 'tinkering is our nature'. Tinkering with Nature is, unfortunately, not always done intelligently enough to avoid its impairment. People are not aware or not aware enough of the consequences of ecologically unsound activities. Many such activities are going on around us causing deforestation, desertification, pollution of air, water, and land, depletion of ozone layer, climatic changes, deterioration of flora and fauna, exhaustion of non-renewable resources etc. The United Nation's Declaration on Human Environment, 1972 cautioned about the environment pollution as: We see around the growing evidence of man-made harm in many regions of the earth. Dangerous level of pollution in water, air, major and undesirable disturbances to ecological balance of the biosphere, destruction and gross deficiencies harmful to the physical, mental and social health of man, in the man-made environment particularly in living and working environment. Further the Stockholm Declaration proclaims that: "Man is both creator and moulder of his environment which gives him physical sustenance and affords him the opportunity for intellectual, moral, social and spiritual growth. In the long and tortuous evolution of the human race on this planet a stage has reached when, through the rapid acceleration of science and technology, man has acquired the power to transform his environment in countless ways and on an unprecedented scale. Both aspects of man's environment, the natural and man-made, are essential to his well-being and to the enjoyment of basic human rights-even the Right to Life itself.

In pursuance of growing environmental concerns, since Stockholm Declaration, one confronts with some important questions i.e. "Where does man stand in the Natural life-web? Is he isolated and totally cut-off from the embrace of environment or he is also a part and parcel of the schema though having a more powerful or dominating status? Has the march of civilization and knowledge created a wide gulf between Nature and Society as a developmental arsenal of science and technology or Is man at the mercy of Nature? How human rights fare in the protection of environment? Should human rights be sacrificed for environment or the two can be mutually compatible for sustainable society? This is very delicate issue demanding deeper perspective and altruistic outlook. Well, there are the tools which may address the problem up to a considerable level. Among them in the very first place is Principle 1 of the Rio-Declaration of the UN Conference on Environment and Development that "human beings are at the centre of concern for sustainable development" and that "they are entitled to a healthy and productive life in harmony with Nature". Secondly, the availability of classic civil and political rights. Their importance lies in their ability to "foster an environmental-friendly political order". Rights to political participation, to life, association, expression, personal liberty, and legal redress would enable those groups who are threatened with environmental degradation to voice their objections. These guarantees are necessary pre-conditions for mobilizing around environmental protection. But, mere prescription of rights and claiming of environmental protection through political rights is not an easy process in practice to achieve a wholesome environment. However it is preferable that existing rights must be reinterpreted with imagination and rigor in context of environmental concerns.

Chapter One elucidates the conceptual framework of human rights, starting from the ancient Doctrine of Natural Rights to American Declaration of Independence, French Declaration of Rights of Man and Citizens and finally to Universal Declaration of Human Rights 1948.

The Second Chapter explains historical evolution of 'Right to Life' under the influence of different political ideologies (in particular, Liberal and Marxist) and its increased recognition after World War-II in United Nations System, regional human rights instruments, and the Constitution of India.

The Third Chapter discusses the relationship between human rights and environment. The overall approach of the chapter is that every human being has 'A human right to healthy environment'. For this purpose international human rights documents, documents on protection of human environment and the relevant provision of the Constitution of India are discussed at length and breadth.

The Fourth Chapter examines the sources, causes and effects of environmental pollution on human health. The whole purpose is to point out the effects of insidious pollutants on human health, which for a common person is beyond his/her imagination under ordinary circumstances.

The Fifth Chapter explains the reasons of unsustainable urbanization and its far-reaching consequences on overall environment, physical as well as social. The Chapter attempts to suggest some guidelines with regard to the vision of sustainable urbanization.

And finally the Conclusion of the book emphasizes that "Man has the fundamental right to freedom, equality and adequate conditions of life, in an environment of a quality that permits a life of dignity and well-being".

1
A Review of Theory of Rights

Life, according to Aristotle, is not merely living but living well.[1] If good life is the aim of man's life, then its pursuit and achievement involves the fulfilment of certain conditions. Rights are those conditions of social life without which man cannot be at his best or give his best, what is needful to the adequate development of his personality and environment. Looked at negatively, rights are those opportunities the absence of which deprives man of something essential. A man without rights, absolutely depends on the daily caprice of a superior authority, is either an animal or a slave. Most generally, right is a special advantage that someone gains because of his or her particular status. The "special advantage" might include gaining a liberty, a power, an entitlement or an immunity. The "particular status" might include one's status as a human being, a woman, a minority, an animal, a child, or a citizen of some country. This general notion of "Right" applies both in legal and moral context. For example in the legal context, if I have the status of being a citizen of India, then I am entitled to the legal rights of any citizen under the Indian Law. In the moral context, if I simply have the status of being human, then I am entitled to human rights that apply to all humans. Also in moral context, if I am an animal, then I am entitled to any animal rights that may apply to animal of my kind.

The concept of human rights is as old as the ancient doctrine of "Natural Rights" founded on Natural Law. This theory of Natural Rights holds that Nature is the author of certain rights that have a universal, rational, eternal and immutable character. Rights being rationally deducible from man's nature, have their universal applications, irrespective of the difference of place, time and environment. The Stoics of ancient Greece upheld the rights to equality as given to us by nature.[2] This school of thought which was initially founded by Zeno of Citium, held the view that a "Universal working force pervades all creations and that human conduct, therefore, should be judged according to and brought into harmony with, the law of nature".[3] The Roman thinkers like Polybius and Cicero emphasized the existence of law of nature to which laws of state must conform. The principles of the law of nature may be understood by man by his rational power. But these principles are of universal and eternal character.

However in the medieval period which roughly ranges from thirteenth century to Treaty of Westphalia (1648), absorbing the period of Renaissance and the decline of feudalism, certain basic changes in the beliefs and the practices of society were seen because people felt the idea of human rights as a general social need. In 1215 A.D. by the Declaration of Magna Carta, the Doctrine of Natural Rights passed into the realm of practical reality when an absolute monarch himself (King John) was made to acknowledge that there were certain rights of the subject which could not be violated even by a Sovereign in whom all powers were legally vested.[4]

The writings of early Christian philosophers in medieval times, foremost among whom was Saint Thomas Aquinas (1224-1274). Thomistic view of Natural Law postulated that it was the part of the God's perfect law which could be divined through the application of human reason.[5] Part of early Natural Law philosophy was the idea that all people –whatever their status – were subjected to the authority of God. From this it was possible to state that not only was the royal authority of monarchs constrained by divine rules, but that all human beings were endowed with a unique individual identity which was separate from the State. Indeed this latter facet of Natural Law doctrine may be seen as containing the seeds of the Natural Rights idea that each person constituted an autonomous individual. Of course, the basis of early Natural Law was entirely theistic, that is, it required belief in the Deity to render it coherent. The next stage in the development of Natural Law, however, was to sever it from its theistic origins and to make it a product of enlightened secular rational thought. This task was undertaken by Dutch jurist *Hugo de Groot* (1583-1665), who is usually known by his Latin name, Grotius, and who is generally acknowledged to be the "Father of International Law". "In his treatise *De lure Belli ac Pacis,* Grotius argued that it was possible to rationalize the existence of Natural Law which was the basis of all positive or written law, on a non-empirical basis by examining the axioms of geometry".[6] Such a mathematical approach to the question of law demonstrated that all rules were ascertainable by the application of 'right reason' and did not depend on the Deity for their validity. This rationalistic, secular approach to law appealed to post-Renaissance scholars, and from the application of Grotian 'right reason' it is possible to discern the development of individual or Natural Rights theory.

However the events like the Petition of Rights (1628) and the English Bill of Rights (1689) testified the increasing popular view that "all human beings are endowed with certain eternal and inalienable rights and they could never be renounced even when humankind contracted to enter the civil society"[7] from that of primitive one, or from the claim of the divine rights of the kings; and thus, the progressive vision of rights took a real meaning as Natural Rights in the 17th and 18th centuries.

The Doctrine of Natural Rights received further impetus at the hands of the great protagonist of the theory of social contract, particularly Locke and Rousseau, who sought to trace the genesis of political society and government in an agreement into which individuals entered to form a collective society to ensure their general interest and objects, but at the same time without interfering with their 'Natural Rights' which already belonged to them as human beings.[8]

Of this group of political thinkers, John Locke, made the most systematic contribution. His Two Treaties of the Government, published in 1690, wielded a great influence on the American colonist in preparing the Declaration of Independence and the written Constitutions. Shorn of details, Locke's theory was that, in the original state of nature, man was governed by the Law of Nature, but for the sake of better safety he joined in a political society by means of a 'social contract' for the mutual preservation of life, liberty and property. The government so set up by a contract was naturally one of limited powers and was bound to the community by the guarantee that the people's Natural Rights would be preserved. The Legislature was thus limited by Natural Law; and a law made by Legislature contrary to the Law of Nature or violative of the Natural Rights of the individual was invalid. The distinct contribution of Locke to the philosophy of Fundamental Rights, thus, was that he did not rest with assertion of the Natural Rights against royal arbitrariness; he held them as against the Legislature as well, even though the 'supreme power in commonwealth' might belong to Legislature.[9] However the critics of Natural Rights theory argue that rights are not abstract, absolute or unidentified phenomena.[10] Though full of contradictions in his philosophy of Social Contract, it was Rousseau who gave kinetic impetus to the doctrine by emphasizing that the sole justification of the State, which derives its authority from the people, was to guarantee the Natural Rights of man, of freedom and equality.[11] These were 'natural' rights in as much as they inhered in man in the 'State of Nature':

"Man is born free and everywhere he is in chains".

It is striking that this concept of Natural Rights, as binding on many political authority, crept into the thoughts of legalist like Blackstone whose writing in 1765[12], made a distinction between absolute and relative rights of persons. By absolute rights of individuals, Blackstone meant- "those which are so in their primary and strictest sense; such as would belong to their persons merely in a state of nature; and which every man is entitled to enjoy, whether out of society or in it". These are to be distinguished from relative rights which are incidental to individuals only as members of society. It is the duty of the political society to protect these absolute rights and, therefore, the State or any authority therein cannot interfere with or encroach upon these Natural Rights except in so far as that is essential for the free maintenance or proper enjoyment of such rights as members of collective society.

Credit must, therefore, go to Blackstone for importing the Doctrine of Natural Rights from the realm of political philosophy into the realm of jurisprudence.[13]

The Virginia Bill of Rights drafted by George Mason[14] and adopted in State Constitution of Virginia in 1776 was the first declaration of rights in a written Constitution "as the basis and foundation of government". The impress of the Doctrine of Natural Rights is to be found in the Preamble of this Declaration:

"All men are by nature equally free and independent and have certain inherent Natural Rights of which when they enter society, they cannot by any contract deprive or divest their posterity...."[15]

The Bill included specific liberties that were to be protected from State interference among them are freedom of press, the free exercise of religion, and the obligation that no person should be deprived of their liberty except by the law of the land or the judgement of their peers.[16]

The Drafters of the US Constitution, influenced by Mason's Virginia Declaration, included the protection of these minimum rights. The Declaration of American Independence, drafted by Jefferson in 1776, said-

"We hold these truths to be self-evident; that all men are created equal; that they are endowed by their creator with certain inalienable rights; that among these are life, liberty, and the pursuit of happiness..."[17]

Though it was not part of the written Constitution, it asserted "certain inalienable rights", as against any government in power, adding that-

"to secure these rights governments are instituted among men, deriving their just powers from consent of the governed."[18]

Inspired by the American Declaration of Independence, the French National Assembly in 1789 formulated the Declaration of the Rights of Man:

The Declaration of the Rights of Man and the Citizens (1789) made it perfectly apparent that government is necessary evil and that as little of it as possible is desirable. According to the Declaration, true happiness is to be found in individual liberty which is the product of 'natural, inalienable and sacred rights of man'. Thus while the Declaration states that certain individual rights are protected- the right to due process, the presumption of innocence, the freedom to hold opinions and religious beliefs , and the freedom to communicate ideas and opinions- it prefaces these with a clear liberation philosophy.

The philosophy underlying this Doctrine of Inalienable Rights, superior to the civil rights, may best be explained in the words of a contemporary political thinker, Thomas Paine:

".....all men are born equal and with equal Natural Rights."[19]

The unmistakable direction in which Americans took a step in advance of the French people in importing the concept of the Inalienable Natural Rights of man into the world of constitutionalism is that they did not stop at reciting these rights in an ornamental Preamble to the Constitution, but adopted them as the part of the Constitution which could serve as the legal limitation on the powers of each of the organs set up by the Constitution like any other mandatory part of that organic instrument and would be enforceable by the Courts to invalidate Legislative and the Executive despotism . Judicial review thus became an inseparable concomitant of the Fundamental Rights.[20]

Whatever the theoretical or doctrinal debates over the basis of English, American and French Revolutions, it is clear that each, in its own way, contributed towards development of forms of liberal democracy in which certain rights were regarded as paramount in protecting individuals from the State's inbuilt tendency to authoritarianism. What was significant about the protected rights was that they were individualistic and libertarian in character: they were predominantly "freedoms from" rather than "rights to."[21] In modern parlance, these would be called civil and political rights, since they dealt primarily with individuals' relationship to the organs of the State. Such was the power of these revolutionary ideas, that there are few modern written constitutions which do not claim to protect these individual rights. In nineteenth century under the influence of German Idealism of Hegel that "State is a march of God on earth"[22] and the rising European nationalism; on the other side of it the Marxian School of thought which is an offshoot of Hegelian thought and dialectical approach, though it did not reject individual rights altogether, but maintained that rights derived from whatsoever source belong to the community or the whole society and not only to individuals.

Among the idealistic school of thought Kant occupies the highest position not only because of his philosophical views but also for his understanding and an explanation of the nature, practice and objective of the rights. For him morality is the force for both the individual and the society. Morality is a factor which establishes an autonomous and an equal status to both of them. Morality is the acting force behind the practical reason. And morality also is the basis of freedom. So rights are nothing but a moral expression of individual actions, and the recognition by the society towards the rights is essentially a moral action and all laws are essentially to be moral in legislation to protect and uphold the freedom of the individual and to him freedom is not only moral but also universal to be exercised by all individuals. He says right is — that totality of conditions, under which the will of one person can be unified with the will of another under a universal law of freedom.[23] For Kant freedom is unconditional so an individual can exercise his free will morally and legally, only when he discharges his duty he becomes a free man. This explains that exercising the right by an individual needs a payment in return by performing and fulfilling his duty which is equally bound by either individual or societal morality.

In early 20th century The Great Economic Depression of the early 1930s struck the first blow at the lofty philosophy of individualism. The social reality came to the force. It was felt that beneath the lofty idealism of Laissez Faire philosophy lay hidden the most ugly aspect of Capitalism.

In the words of Julius Stone

"The fallacy of supposing that a workman, living from hand to mouth on daily labour in the same way as a great commercial or industrial corporation resents restrictions on its free bargaining is now well recognized."

The fact of the matter is that the working class was as much a product of Industrial Revolution as the Fundamental Rights. As Capitalism reached its zenith, a sad realization dawned on human beings that in their actual working, Fundamental Rights became the rights of capitalist class alone: for the working class they carried no meaning. The Economic Depression revealed that though the ideology of Laissez Faire triumphed, its end-product was divided society, divided between privileged and underdogs. The Capitalism which once fought against the vested interests of feudalism, itself acquired vested interests. Sadly, in the words of President Roosevelt; "one third of our population, the overwhelming of which is in industry and agriculture is ill-nourished, ill-clad and ill-housed."[24]

The State of affairs led to some rethinking. It was felt that Laissez Faire works hardships when men are not equal. No democratic state could tolerate this ignoring state of affairs where the weak were continually driven to wall. A feeling generated that if Fundamental Rights were to have any meaning to the millions, their content must change. If rights were considered as conditions necessary for the fulfillment of life, then the working class too, should have these rights guaranteed to them. The resultant effect was the emergence of new rights known as "Social and Economic Rights". It includes the right to work, right to employment, right to leisure, right to public assistance in case of unemployment, old age or sickness, right to collective bargaining, right to education etc. However, a trend to include those rights as part of Bill of Rights started only in post world war era. In the Weimer Republican Constitution and the Constitution of USSR these rights were recognized as Fundamental Rights.[25] In modern Constitutions of many States these rights in some form or the other, are also recognized, though grudgingly, guardedly and with "ifs" and "buts".

The history of the almost entire first half of twentieth century is characterized by the prevalence of colonial rule in large parts of the world, the rise of authoritarian governments in many countries and the establishment of fascist, barbarous and aggressive regimes in some countries on one hand and the rise of national liberation movements in the colonies and of movements of democracy and social progress in various countries on the other. The twentieth century also saw the two most devastating wars in the human history- the twenty years of 'peace' between the two being mainly a period of preparation for the Second World War. Because of this, the period from 1914, when the First World War broke out, to 1945 when the Second World War ended, has been described as the Age of Catastrophe.[26] It was during the closing years of this Age of Catastrophe, during the war against fascism in Germany and Italy and World War-II, the conceptualization and articulation of human rights took place.

The United Nations Declaration of January 1, 1942, put on record that complete victory over their enemies is essential to defend life, liberty, independence and religious freedom, and to preserve human rights and justice in their own land as well as in other lands. The Big Three (United States, Soviet Union and Great Britain) endorsed the above Declaration in their Conference of March 3, 1943.[27] Then came the Philadelphia Declaration of the International Labour Organization's 26th session, which laid down:

"All human beings, irrespective of trade, creed or sex, have the right to pursue both their material well-being and their spiritual development in conditions of freedom and dignity of economic security and equal opportunity."[28]

The Dumbarton Oaks Conference of 1944 among the four Big Powers led to the first tentative draft of a new world organization.[29] At Yalta Conference of 1945, the Great Powers issued a declaration of liberated Europe where principles of Atlantic Charter and Declaration of United Nations were affirmed.

Then came on April 25, 1945 the San Francisco Conference of the United Nations where the Charter of United Nations emerged.[30] The Charter of the United Nations began with the following words:

"We, The People of The United Nations, determined to save succeeding generations from the scourge of war which twice in our lifetime has brought untold sorrow to mankind, and to reaffirm faith in fundamental human rights, in the dignity and worth of the human person, in the equal rights of men and women and of nations large and small, and to establish conditions under which justice and respect for the obligations arising from treaties and other sources of international law can be maintained, and to promote social progress and better standard of life in larger freedom..."[31].

Three years after UN Charter, The Universal Declaration of Human Rights (1948) was proclaimed. The Declaration furnished an elaborate universal statement on human rights. The UN General Assembly proclaimed the Declaration as a 'common standard of achievement for all people and all nations', which all members have to observe and enforce. At the time of the adoption of the Declaration by the General Assembly, none voted against it. That itself shows the importance of the Declaration. From this brief historical exposition, it will be apparent that the notion of human rights has made a transition from exclusive concern with the protection of Individual from State absolutism to the creation of social and economic conditions calculated to allow the individual to develop to the maximum of his or her potential. As Szabo[32] puts it, the purpose of human rights is to 'defend by institutionalized means the rights of human beings against abuses of power committed by the organs of State and, at the same time to promote the multi-dimensional development of the human personality'.

CONCLUSION

In the words of Maurice Cranston it is certainly true that some rights are more difficult to secure than others, and those that are impossible to secure cannot truly be called rights. And it is true that some rights (such as the right not to be subjected to torture) seems to be more important than others (like the right to paid vacations). Secondly, if we all sincerely ascribe to the concept of universality of human rights, we are all compelled to join efforts in ensuring the promotion and preservation of human rights. The human rights crisis in many developing countries and the sad state of development therein cannot just be the problem and concern of developing countries. This fact was highlighted by none other than Nelson Mandela in his speech to United Nations General Assembly when he said," No people could truly say they were blessed with happiness, peace and prosperity when others continued to be afflicted with misery, armed conflict, terrorism and deprivation".

REFERENCES

1. Anup Chand Kapur, *Principles of Political Science*, New Delhi, S. Chand and Company Ltd., 1996, p 222.

2. As cited by J.C.Johari, *Principles of Modern Political Science*, New Delhi, Sterling Publishers Pvt. Ltd. 1989, p 178.
3. Richard Pierre Claude and H.Weston Burns, *Human Rights in the World Community: Issues and Actions,* Philadelphia: University of Pennsylvania Press, 1989.
4. D.D. Basu, *Human Rights in Constitutional Law*, New Delhi, Prentice Hall of India Pvt.Ltd., 1994, p 42.
5. As cited by Scott. Davidson, *Human Rights*, Philadelphia Open University Press, 1993, p 27.
6. *Ibid.*
7. Arun Kumar Palai, *National Human Rights Commission of India, formation, functioning and future prospects*, New Delhi , Khana Publishers, 1998, p 3.
8. Rousseau, *Social Contract*, 1762(Everyman), I , p (vi).
9. D.D. Basu, *Op.cit* , p 43.
10. J.C. Johari, *Op. cit*, 1989, p 176.
11. Rousseau, *Social Contract*, 1762(Everyman), I , i ; Discourse on Inequality, Pt. II.
12. Blackstone, *(1765) I Comm. Chap.I*, pp 123-25 (Coleridge Ed.)
13. *Ibid*. Book I, Chap.2, pp. 161-62.
14. Scott. Davidson, *Op.cit,* p 3.
15. D.D. Basu, *Op.cit*, p 44.
16. Scott Davidson, *Op.cit*, p 3.
17. D.D. Basu, *Op.cit*, p 44.
18. *Ibid*, p 45.
19. Thomas Paine, *Rights of Man* (1791-92), (1958 Everyman Ed.), pp. 42,44-45.
20. D.D. Basu, *Op.cit,* p 46.
21. Paras Diwan , Peeyushi Diwan , *Human Rights and The Law*, New Delhi, Deep and Deep Publications, 1996,p 6.

22. R.C. Agarwal, *Political Theory*, New Delhi, S.Chand and Company Ltd., 1997, p 186.
23. Paul Guyer, *The Cambridge Companion to Kant*, USA, Cambridge University Press, 1993, p 344.
24. Paras Diwan, Peeyushi Diwan, *Human Rights and The Law*, New Delhi, Deep and Deep Publications, 1996, p 7.
25. *Ibid*. p 8.
26. Arjun Dev, Indira Arjun Dev, Supta Das, *Human Rights 'A Source Book'*, NCERT, 1996, p (xii).
27. Paras Diwan, *Op.cit*, p 24.
28. *Ibid*, p 24.
29. *Ibid.*
30. Paras Diwan, *Op.cit*, p 24
31. Arjun Dev, *Op.cit*, p (xiii).
32. Scott Davidson, *Op.cit*, p 7.

2
Evolution of Right to Life

The Right to Life is most fundamental of all the rights, as it is the very core of humanity. The nearest dictionary meaning of life is that life is the state of being alive as a human being, it also means the qualities, events and experiences of human existence.[1]

In the history of political thought, the notion of human rights is a relatively recent innovation tracing its roots to the social contract thinkers, such as Thomas Hobbes and John Locke, who emphasized during the seventeenth and eighteenth centuries that individuals possess certain Natural Rights that serve as basis of political order and that may not be legitimately revoked by governments. This revolutionary concept served as the foundation upon which the great statements of individual rights and liberties - the American Declaration of Independence and the French Declaration on the Rights of Man - were based.

Aristotle in his "Politics" while explaining the origin and end of State observed that State came into being for fulfilment of bare needs of men and continues in existence for the sake of good life.[2] If good life is the aim of man's life, then, its pursuit and achievement involves the fulfilment of certain conditions.

Credit must go to Hobbes for justifying man's natural right to life, for him, Natural Rights begin as a claim which everyone naturally makes. Nobody wants to die a violent death, or to suffer an injury. Therefore, the desire to stay alive is, generally speaking, man's paramount wish, and the one that demands from other their most unfailing respect. To say that man has a Right to Life is to convert that demand into a kind of moral imperative, that is to impose on all men a reciprocal duty to abstain from injuring their neighbours. Hobbes's 'social contract' formulation further strengthened the concept of Right to Life in a politically organized society i.e. State. In fact Hobbes's Leviathan came into being due to this contract whereby it undertakes to protect the rights of the people.[3]

Locke's theory was that, in the original state of nature, man was governed by the Law of Nature, but for the sake of better safety he joined in a political society by means of a 'social contract' for the mutual preservation of life, liberty and property. The distinct contribution of Locke to the philosophy of Fundamental Rights was that he did not rest with assertion of the Natural Rights against royal arbitrariness; he held them as against the Legislature as well, even though the 'supreme power in commonwealth' might belong to Legislature. Both government and society exist to preserve the individuals' rights, and indefensibility of such rights is a limitation on the authority of both.[4] Therefore, in one part of Locke's theory, the individual and his rights figure as ultimate principles. In fact, the expression which he commonly used to enumerate Natural Rights was right to "life, liberty, and estate". These three enumerated rights can never justly be set aside, since society itself exists to protect them. However, the right to "life, liberty and estate" of one person can be limited only to make effective the equally valid claims of another person to the same right.[5] Hence, Locke recognised the Right to Life and emphasised its protection by State itself.

Rousseau on the other hand draws fascinating picture of state of nature and glorifies Natural Rights. While explaining 'Social Contract' Rousseau stresses upon the need of 'the total alienation of each associate together with all his rights to the whole community'.[6] The clause of alienation of all the rights does not, however, mean the alienation of the Natural Rights of men. Rousseau clearly distinguishes between the "rights of the citizens and the sovereign and between the duties the former have to fulfil as subjects. Indeed, the purpose of the State is to protect those rights that individual cannot defend on their own. The craving for rights was initially a Doctrine of Social Philosophy which has since entered into political and captured the constitutional field. Historically, the violent revolutions perpetrated in the wake of social and political consciousness, have secured to the individual his Natural Rights which had long been denied to him. The principle of equality had been the central theme of this concept, but in ancient period, its significance was metaphysical which confined itself to the Episcopal authority of the church till the medieval period.

In England, the success of the Glorious Revolution of 1689 was the drive for the respect for Fundamental Rights. On the outset, the Declaration of Rights was codified into the Bill of Rights, 1689. The 18th century witnessed the American War of Independence after which the Declaration of Independence of U.S.A. in 1976 declared the right to life, liberty and pursuit of happiness as inalienable rights.[7] Thereafter, in 1791, by virtue of First Ten Amendments in the form of Bill of Rights, the Americans were the first nation to incorporate Fundamental Rights in their Constitution. At the same time, French also arose from their own slumber and the Declaration of the Rights of Man and Citizens was adopted in the French Revolution of 1789.[8]

The Declaration of the Rights of Man and the Citizens (1789) made it perfectly apparent that government is necessary evil, and that as little of it as possible is desirable. According to the Declaration, true happiness is to be found in individual liberty which is the product of natural, inalienable and sacred rights of man. The Doctrine of Inalienable Rights, superior to the civil rights, may best be explained in the words of a contemporary political thinker, Thomas Paine : "... All men are born equal and with equal Natural Rights".[9]

The unmistakable direction in which Americans took a step

in advance of the French people in importing the concept of the Inalienable Natural Rights of man into the world of constitutionalism is that they do not stop at reciting these rights in an ornamental Preamble to the Constitution, but adopted them as a part of the Constitution which could serve as a legal limitation on the powers of each of the organs set up by the Constitution like any other mandatory part of that organic instrument and would be enforceable by the courts to invalidate Legislative and Executive acts that might transgress these inalienable rights.[10] By World War I, there were scarcely any theorists who would or could defend the "Rights of Man" along the lines of Natural Law. Indeed, under the influence of German Idealism and parallel expressions of rising European nationalism, there were some - the Marxists, for example - who, although not rejecting individualism altogether, maintained that rights from whatever source derived belong to communities or whole societies and nations pre-eminently.[11] Thus did F.H. Bradely, the British Idealist, wrote in 1894 : "The rights of the individual are today not worth serious consideration - the welfare of the community is the end and is the ultimate standard".[12]

Whatever the theoretical or doctrinal debates over the bases for the English, American and French Revolutions, it is clear that each, in its own way, contributed towards the development of forms of liberal democracy in which certain rights were regarded as paramount in protecting individuals from the States inbuilt tendency to authoritarianism. What was significant about the protected rights was that they were individualistic and libertarian in character : they were predominantly 'freedom from' rather than 'rights to'.[13] In modern parlance, these would be called civil and political rights, since they dealt primarily with individuals' relationship to the organs of the State.

Civil and political rights are not, however, the only rights which are protected by modern constitutions and contemporary international law. A variety of economic, social and cultural and other rights are also the subjects of various forms of protection. The Great Economic Depression of the early 1930s struck the first blow at the lofty philosophy of individualism. It was felt that beneath the lofty idealism of Laissez Faire philosophy lay hidden the most ugly aspect of Capitalism. The Economic Depression revealed that though the ideology of Laissez Faire triumphed, its end-product was a divided society, divided between privileged and underdogs. The Capitalism which once fought against the vested interests of feudalism, itself acquired vested interests.[14] The state of affairs led to some rethinking. It was felt that Laissez Faire works hardships, when men are not equal. No democratic state could tolerate this ignoring state of affairs where the weak were continually driven to wall. A feeling generated that if Fundamental Rights were to have any meaning to the millions, their content must change. If rights were considered conditions necessary for the fulfilment of life, then working class too, shall have these rights guaranteed to them. The resultant effect was the emergence of new rights known as "Social and Economic Rights".[15] Karal Vasak, French jurist gives them the name of second-generation rights.[16]

In the Weimer Republican Constitution and the Constitution of USSR these rights were recognised as Fundamental Rights.[17] In modern Constitutions of many States these rights, in some form or the other, are also recognised though grudgingly, guardedly and with 'ifs' and 'buts'.

From this brief historical exposition, it is apparent that the notion of human rights has made a transition from exclusive concern with the protection of the individual from State absolutism to the creation of social and economic conditions calculated to allow the individual to develop to the maximum of his or her potential. As Szabo puts it, the purpose of human rights is to 'defend by institutionalized means the rights of human beings against the abuse of power committed by the organs of the State and at the same time to promote the multi-dimensional development of human personality'.[18]

It is the same mainstream which, after the horrors of World War Second, found expression in the UN Charter 1945 and in the Universal Declaration of Human Rights of 1948.

HUMAN RIGHTS IN THE UNITED NATIONS

The Charter of the United Nations (1945) begins by reaffirming a "faith in fundamental human rights, in the dignity and worth of the human person, in the equal rights of men and women and of nations large and small".[19] It states that the purposes of the United Nations is, among other things, "to develop friendly relations among nations based on respect for the principle of equal rights and self-determination of peoples[20]... [and] to achieve international co-operation.... in promoting and encouraging respect for human rights and fundamental freedom for all without distinction as to race, sex, language, or religion...".[21] And, in two key articles, all members "pledge themselves to take joint and separate action in cooperation with the Organisation" for the achievement of these and related purposes.[22]

THE UNIVERSAL DECLARATION OF HUMAN RIGHTS

Three years after UN Charter, the Universal Declaration of Human Rights was adopted by the General Assembly on December 10, 1948.[23] The catalog of rights set out in the Universal Declaration of Human Rights, is scarcely less than the sum of all the important traditional political and civil rights of national constitutions and legal systems, including equality before law; right to an adequate standard of living ...... More importantly the Right to Life proclaimed in the Universal Declaration of Human Rights says in Article 3 that "Everyone has the right to life, liberty and security of person. The meaning and scope of the Right to Life is clarified in the International Covenant of Civil and Political Rights[24] in the following provisions:

Article 6(1) Every human being has the inherent Right to Life. This right shall be protected by law. No one shall be arbitrarily deprived of his life. On December 18, 1982, the United Nations General Assembly adopted a resolution in which it expressed its firm conviction that all peoples and all individuals have an inherent right to life and safeguarding of this foremost right is an essential condition for the enjoyment of the entire range of economic, social and cultural as well as civil and political rights. The General Assembly, therefore, requested the Commission on Human Rights, in its future activities, to stress the need to ensure the cardinal right of everyone to life, liberty and security of person, and to live in peace.[25]

The Commission of Human Rights in its resolution 1982/7 adopted on 19 February 1982, expressed its firm conviction that all people and all individuals have an inherent Right to Life, and that safeguarding of this foremost right is an essential condition for the enjoyment of the entire range of economic, social and cultural, as well as civil and political rights. The Commission repeated these statements in its resolution 1983/43 adopted on 9 March 1983. In the latter resolution, the Commission stated that 'for people in the world today there is no more important question than that of preserving peace and ensuring cardinal right of every human being, namely, the Right to Life'.

International concern for human rights has also been evident outside the United Nations. For example, The American Convention on Human Rights[26]; the European Convention for the Protection of Human Rights and Fundamental Freedoms[27], which first met in 1950; and the Organization of African Unity in 1981 adopted the African Charter on Human and Peoples' Rights.[28]

THE AMERICAN CONVENTION ON HUMAN RIGHTS

Article 4(1) of the Convention provides that "every person has the right to have his life respected. This right shall be protected by law and, in general, from the moment of conception. No one shall be arbitrarily deprived of his life".

THE EUROPEAN CONVENTION OF HUMAN RIGHTS

Article 2(1) of the Convention provides that "everyone's Right to Life shall be protected by law. No one shall be deprived of his life intentionally save in the execution of a sentence of a court following his conviction of a crime for which his penalty is provided by law".

THE AFRICAN CHARTER ON HUMAN AND PEOPLES' RIGHTS

Article 4 of the Convention provides that "human beings are inviolable. Every human being shall be entitled to respect for his life and the integrity of his person. No one may be arbitrarily deprived of this right".

THE CONSTITUTION OF INDIA

The inclusion of a set of Fundamental Rights, which are necessary for the development and efflorescence of human personality, in the Constitution of India had its genesis in the forces that operated in the national movement for independence during the British rule.

Perhaps one first explicit demand for Fundamental Rights appeared in the Constitution of India Bill, 1895[29] which envisaged for India a Constitution guaranteeing to every citizen of India, freedom of expression, right to equality before law, right to personal liberty etc. It was the consistent effort of the leaders of our freedom movement which led the British Cabinet Mission in 1946 to recognize the need for a written guarantee of Fundamental Rights in the Constitution of India. In paragraph 19 and 20 of its statement of May 16, 1946, envisaging a Constituent Assembly for framing the Constitution of India. It recommended the setting up of an Advisory Committee for reporting the Assembly *inter-alia* on Fundmental Rights.[30]

Therefore, Constituent Assembly of 296 members as envisaged under the Cabinet mission proposal was formed to frame the Indian Constitution. The Constituent Assembly on 24

January 1947 voted to form the Advisory Committee. Sardar Patel became the chairman of the Advisory Committee. The Advisory Committee in turn set up five sub-committees out of which one was the sub-committee on Fundamental Rights. Acharya Kripalani became the chairman of this sub-committee. When the Fundamental Rights sub-committee met for the first time on 27 February 1947, it had before it draft list of rights, as well as miscellaneous notes and memoranda on various aspects of rights. The Fundamental Rights sub-committee was faced with a problem of balancing the individual liberty vis-a-vis social control. The former being necessary for fulfilment of individual's personality and latter for peace and stability of the society. The sub-committee discussed the subject of "Right to Life and Liberty" on March 25th, 26th and 27th, 1947 and included in its draft report two clauses 11th and 29th viz.

11th No person shall be deprived of his life, liberty or property without 'Due Process of Law'.

29th No person shall be subject to prolonged detention pending trial, excessive bail or unreasonable refusal thereof or inhuman or cruel punishment.

Commenting on the draft report Sir B.N. Rau, Constitutional Advisor, pointed out that clause 11 had been adopted from 5th and 14th amendments of American Constitution. Clause 29 was based on Article 1 of the Lanterpacht's 'An International Bill of Rights of Man', and 6th and 8th amendments of American Constitution. When the sub-committee met on April 14 and 15, 1947, to consider draft report in the light of comments received, it reaffirmed its recommendations to incorporate both clauses 11 and 29, in the Indian Constitution. However after so many debates over the phrase 'due process of law' the Drafting Committee on January 19, 1948 decided to replace the expression 'due process of law' by the expression, 'except according to procedure established by law'. The latter expression which the committee considered was more specific in its import was borrowed from Article 31 of the Japanese Constitution. The text of the provision thus recast by the Committee was incorporated in Article 15 of the Draft Constitution.

"No person shall be deprived of his life or personal liberty except according to procedure established by law, nor shall any person be denied equality before law or equal protection of laws within the territory of India".[31]

On December 13, 1948, the Article is again discussed. Dr. B.R. Ambedkar makes the following statement:

"We are placed in two difficult positions. One is to give the judiciary the authority to sit in judgement over the will of Legislature and to question the law made by the Legislature on the ground that it is not good law, in consonance with Fundamental Principles. Is that a desirable principle ? The second position is that Legislature ought to be trusted not to make bad laws. It was very difficult to come to any definite conclusion."[32]

After so many discussions the Constituent Assembly finally adopted Article 15 in the following words:

"No person shall be deprived of his life or personal liberty, except according to procedure established by law". This became Article 21 in the Constitution of India".

CONCLUSION

The Right to Life at 'national' and 'international' level is the most fundamental and primordial right which inspires or informs all other rights, from which latter obtain *raison d'être* and take their lead. Thus it is very important that 'right' be carefully defined and that its elements and characteristics be scrupulously analysed.

The economic, social, cultural and political rights come into existence only when an individual is capable of living. These rights under any circumstance can't come into practice by the lapse of Right to Life which is the essence of mankind. Right to

Life does not mean simply putting body and soul together, it includes the optimum possible decent and good life for the individual both as a person and as well as a member of the human community.

If the Right to Life is the supreme right, States have the supreme duty with reference to the protection of this right, in effect of which, and according to article 4 of the Covenant (ICCPR), the Right to Life is non-derogable in any condition. Non-derogability of the Right to Life should be considered as the formal protective element which is included in the States' obligations under both national and international law.

REFERENCES

1. *Oxford Advanced Learners Dictionary*, Hornby, A.S., 5th Edition (Oxford : Oxford University Press, 1995), p. 680.
2. E. Barker, *The Political Thought of Plato and Aristotle*, Dover Publications, New York, 1959, p. 281.
3. Maurice Cranston, *What are Human Rights* ?, The Bodley Head Ltd., London, 1973, pp. 25-26.
4. George H. Sabine, *A History of Political Theory*, Oxford and JBH Publishing Co., Delhi, 1961, pp. 525-526.
5. *Ibid.*
6. R.G. Chaturvedi, *State and Rights of Men*, Metropolitan Book Co. Pvt. Ltd., Delhi, 1971, p. 148.
7. *Ibid.*, p. 5.
8. *Ibid.*
9. Thomas Paine, "*Rights of Man*" (1791-92), (1958 Everyman Ed.), pp. 42, 44-45.
10. Board of Education (1943) 319 U.S. 624 (638).
11. *Encyclopaedia of Britannica*, 15th Edition, 1985, Vol. 20, p. 657.
12. *Ibid.*

13. Scott Davidson, *Human Rights*, Philadelphia Open University Press, 1993, p. 6.

14. Paras Diwan, Peeyushi Diwan, *Human Rights and Law*, New Delhi, Deep and Deep Publications, 1996, p. 6.

15. *Ibid.*

16. Scott Davidson, *Op.cit.*, p. 6.

17. Paras Diwan, *Op.cit.*, p. 8.

18. Scott Davidson, *Op.cit.*, p. 7.

19. Preamble, UN Charter, June 26, 1945, 59 Stat. 1031, T.S. 993, 3 Bevans, 1153 entered into force Oct. 24, 1945.

20. Article 1, *Op.cit.*

21. Article 55, *Op.cit.*

22. Article 56, *Op.cit.*.

23. General Assembly Resolution 217(III), U.N. Doc. A/810 at 71 (1948).

24. G.A. Resolution 2200 A (XXI), 21 U.N. GAOR Supp. (No. 16) at 52, U.N. Doc A/6316 (1966), 999 U.N.T.S. 171, entered into force March 23, 1976.

25. General Assembly Resolution 37/189A, paras 1 and 6.

26. American Convention on Human Rights, O.A.S. Treaty Series No. 36, 1144 U.N.T.S. 123 entered into force July 18, 1978.

27. European Convention for the Protection of Human Rights and Fundamental Freedom, 213 U.N.T.S. 222, entered into force September 3, 1953.

28. African Charter on Human and Peoples' Rights, adopted June 27, 1981, OAU Doc CAB/LEG/67/3 rev. 5, 21 I.L.M. 58 (1982), entered into force Oct. 21, 1986.

29. The Constitution of India Bill, 1895, B. Shiva Rao, *The Framing of India's Constitution, Select Documents*, Vol. 1, The Indian Institute of Public Administration, New Delhi, 1966, pp. 5-14.

30. Gwyer, Maurice and Appadorai, A., *Speeches and Documents on the Indian Constitution*, Oxford University Press, London, 1957, p. 283.
31. Constituent Assembly Debates, Lok Sabha Secretariat, (1948-49), Vol. III, p. 842.
32. *Ibid.*, pp. 999-1001.

3

Right to Life and Environment

Life means to live with human dignity but if one can not breathe clean air, have safe drinking water or healthy food, then talk of all human rights is useless.

The environmental dimension of human rights is recognised by the ever-increasing support for right to a healthy environment, since 1968 an increasing number of international declarations and statements have, with growing specificity recognised the fundamental connection between the environmental protection and the respect for human rights. In 1968 the UN General Assembly passed a resolution identifying the relationship between the quality of the human environment and the enjoyment of basic rights.[1] This was followed in 1972 by the landmark Stockholm Declaration, Principle 1 of the *Stockholm Declaration* established a foundation for linking human rights and environmental protection, declaring that man has a Fundamental Right to freedom, equality and adequate conditions of life, in an environment of quality that permits a life of dignity and well-being.[2] It also announced the responsibility of each person to protect and improve the environment for present and future generations. More recently the Hague Declaration stated that "the Right to Life is the paramount duty of those in charge of all states throughout the world".[3] With the passage of time environmental protection began to find place in the agenda of International Organisations. Stockholm Conference gave an impetus to the nations to think that environment has to be protected for facilitating the Right to Life.

Clean Environment as the right of human beings began to find a place in some regional treaties. Article 24 of the African Charter on Human and People's Rights (1981) expressly provide that "all people have right to a general satisfactory environment, favourable to their development".

In 1990, the UN General Assembly declared that "all individuals are entitled to live in an environment adequate for their health and well-being".[4] The United Nations Commission on Human Rights also adopted a resolution in 1990, entitled "Human Rights and the Environment", which again reaffirmed the relationship between preservation of environment and the promotion of human rights.[5]

In a build-up period to the 1992 Rio Conference on Environment and Development there have been many proposals to institutionalize a right to decent environment. The Draft Earth Charter is one of them.[6] However the eventually adopted Rio Declaration relates the rights issue to the broader issue of sustainable development. This is expressed in Principle 1: "Human beings are at the centre of concerns for sustainable development. They are entitled to a healthy and productive life in harmony with nature". In contrast, the Right to Development is clearly spelled out.[7] At the European level, recognition of an environmental human right is more emphatic. The Organization for Economic Cooperation and Development (OECD) stated that Fundamental Human Rights should include a right to "decent" environment.[8] More recently in the Charter on Environmental Rights and Obligations drafted by the United Nations Economic Commission for Europe (UNECE), which affirms the right of everyone to an environment adequate for general health and well-being and the responsibility to protect and conserve the environment for present and future generations.[9]

An important indicator of the environmental human right is the extent to which it has emerged in national constitutions. A number of studies exist which list these constitutional provisions.[10] Generally speaking, they reveal that more than national constitutions, from a variety of legal traditions, include an environmental human right.[11] As two commentators point out, virtually every constitution revised or adopted since 1970 has addressed environmental issues.[12] One of the most frequently cited constitutional provision is from the new Brazilian Constitution, which states that : "everybody has a right to an ecologically balanced environment, an asset for common use by the people, and essential to the wholesome quality of life. This imposes upon Public Authorities and the Community the obligation to defend and preserve it for present and future generations".[13]

DECISIONS AND COMMENTS OF EUROPEAN HUMAN RIGHTS BODIES

The major decision of the Court on environmental harm as a breach of the right to private life and the home is *Lopez-Ostra v. Spain*.[14] The applicant and her daughter suffered serious health problems from the fumes of a tannery waste treatment plant which operated alongside the apartment building where they lived. The plant opened in July 1988 without a required license and without having followed the procedure for obtaining such a license. The plant malfunctioned when it began operations, releasing gas fumes and contaminants, which immediately caused health problems and nuisance to people living in the district. The town council evacuated the local residents and rehoused them free of charge in the town center during the summer. Inspite of this, the authorities allowed the plant to resume partial operation. In October the applicant and her family returned to their flat where there were continuing problems. The applicant finally sold her house and moved in 1992.

The decision is significant for several reasons. First, the Court did not require the applicant to exhaust administrative remedies to challenge operation of the plant under the environmental protection laws, but only to complete remedies applicable to enforcement of basic rights. Mrs. Lopez exhausted the latter remedies when the Supreme Court of Spain denied her appeal on a suit for infringement of her Fundamental Rights and her complaint with the Constitutional Court was dismissed as manifestly ill-founded. Two sisters-in-law of Mrs Lopez Ostra, who lived in the same building as her, followed the procedures concerning environmental law. They brought administrative proceedings alleging that the plant was operating unlawfully. On 18 September 1991 the local court, noting a continuing nuisance and that the plant did not have the licenses required by law, ordered that it should be closed until they were obtained. However, enforcement of this order was stayed following an appeal. The case was still pending in the Supreme Court in 1995 when the European Court issued its judgment. The two sisters-in-law also lodged a complaint, as a result of which a local judge instituted criminal proceedings against the plant for an environmental health offence. The two complainants joined the proceedings as civil parties.

The European Human Rights Court noted that severe environmental pollution may affect individuals' well-being and prevent them from enjoying their homes in such a way as to affect their private and family life adversely, without, however, seriously endangering their health. It found that the determination of whether this violation had occurred should be tested by striking a fair balance between the interest of the town's economic well-being and the applicant's effective enjoyment of her right to respect for her home and her private and family life. In doing this, the Court applied its Margin of Appreciation Doctrine, allowing the State certain discretion in determining the appropriate balance, but finding in this case that the Margin of Appreciation had been exceeded. It awarded Mrs. Lopez 4,000,000 pesetas, plus costs and attorney's fees.

In *Anna Maria Guerra and 39 others against Italy* [15] the applicants complained of pollution resulting from operation of the chemical factory 'ENICHEM Agricoltura,' situated near the town of Manfredonia; the risk of major accidents at the plant; and the absence of regulation by the public authorities. Invoking

Article 10 of the European Convention on Human Rights, the applicants asserted in particular the government's failure to inform the public of the risks and the measures to be taken in case of a major accident, prescribed by the domestic law transposing the EC 'Seveso' directive.[16] The former European Commission on Human Rights[17] admitted the complaint insofar as it alleged a violation of the right to information. It did not accept the claim of pollution damage. Most of the facts were uncontested. The Commission found that the government had classified the factory as a "high risk" facility in applying the criteria established by the EC directive and Italian law and that there had been accidents at the factory, including an explosion that sent more than 150 persons to the hospital. A technical commission named by the city of Manfredonia found that according to the factory's own study the treatment of emissions was inadequate and the environmental impact study incomplete. During the operations of the chemical factory, the government instigated several inquiries. In addition, the residents of Manfredonia instituted civil actions. The Commission nonetheless found that the law was inadequately enforced, giving the company almost complete impunity to pollute. In addition to its failure to hold the company responsible for polluting, the government took no action between the adoption of the "Seveso" law and the cessation of chemical production by the factory in 1994 to inform the population of the situation or to make operational a contingency plan.

The decision centered on the interpretation of state duties under Article 10. The applicants insisted that they sought information from the government that was not otherwise available to them. The government in turn claimed that the law protected industrial secrets, prohibiting authorities from divulging such information in their possession. The essential question before the Commission was whether the right to information for the directly concerned public imposed on the government a positive duty to inform.

By a large majority, the Commission concluded that Article 10 imposes on states the positive duty to collect, collate, and disseminate information which would otherwise not be directly accessible to the public or brought to the public's attention. In arriving at its conclusion, the Commission relied upon "the present state of European law" (l'état actuel du droit européen) which it said confirmed that public information represents one of the essential instruments for protecting the well-being and health of the populace in situations of environmental danger. The Commission referred specifically to the Chernobyl Resolution, adopted by the Parliamentary Assembly of the Council of Europe, which it said recognized, at least in Europe, a fundamental right to information concerning activities that are dangerous for the environment or human well-being.

The case was referred to a Grand Chamber of the European Court of Human Rights, which issued its judgment on February 19, 1998. The Court reversed the Commission on its expanded reading of Article 10, but unanimously found a violation of Article 8, the right to family, home and private life. The Court reaffirmed its earlier case law holding that Article 10 generally only prohibits a government from interfering with a person's freedom to receive information that others are willing to impart. According to the Court, that freedom cannot be construed as imposing on a State, in circumstances such as those of the present case, positive obligations to collect and disseminate information of its own motion.[18] Eight of the 20 judges suggested in separate opinions that positive obligations to collect and disseminate information might exist in some circumstances.

In regard to Article 8, the Court reaffirmed that it can impose positive obligations on states to ensure respect for private or family life. Citing the *Lopez Ostra* case, the Court reiterated that severe environmental pollution may affect individuals' well-being and prevent them from enjoying their homes in such a way as to affect their private and family life.[19] Noting that the individuals waited throughout the operation of fertilizer production at the company for essential information that would have enabled them to assess the risks they and their families might run if they continued to live at Manfredonia, a town particularly exposed to danger in the event of an accident at the factory, the Court found a violation of Article 8.

The Court appears to have strained to avoid overturning its prior case law interpreting Article 10. The basis of the complaint was the government's failure to provide environmental information, not pollution like that found in the *Lopez-Ostra* case. The Court also declined to consider whether the Right to Life guaranteed by Article 2 had been violated, considering it unnecessary in light of its decision on Article 8, despite the fact that deaths from cancer had occurred in the factory and this would have a clear bearing on damages. In regard to the latter, the Court found that applicants had not proved pecuniary damages but were entitled to ITL 10,000,000 each for non-pecuniary damage. The applicants also sought a clean-up order, which the Court declined to give on the ground that it lacks the power to issue orders

The right to a remedy extends to compensation for pollution. In the European case *Zimmerman and Steiner v. Switzerland* [20] , the Court found Article 6 applicable to a complaint about the length of proceedings for compensation for injury caused by noise and air pollution from a nearby airport. Article 6 does not, however, encompass a right to judicial review of legislative enactments.

The European Court of Human Rights has legitimised environmental restrictions on the use of private property. A 1991 Court decision, *Pine Valley Developments Limited and Others v. Ireland*, continues this trend.[21] In Pine Valley, the applicants complained that the denial by local planning authorities of permission to construct commercial buildings on their land constituted a violation of Protocol I, Article 1. Permission to build was denied because the area was zoned as a green belt. The Court concluded that, although the planning restrictions constituted an interference with the right to peaceful enjoyment, the interference did not constitute a violation of Protocol I, Article 1, because it was lawful, in pursuit of a legitimate aim and proportionate to that aim. The Court stated that preventing construction "for the further development of agriculture so as to preserve a green belt must be regarded as a proper way if not the only way of achieving that aim". This case thus demonstrates that environmental concerns are encompassed within the human rights instruments.

Nearly all global and regional human rights bodies have considered the link between environmental degradation and internationally-guaranteed human rights. In nearly every instance, the complaints brought have not been based upon a specific right to a safe and environmentally-sound environment, but rather upon rights to life, property, health, information, family and home life. Underlying the complaints, however, are instances of pollution, deforestation, water pollution, and other types of environmental harm. It may be asked whether or not a recognized and explicit right to a safe and environmentally-sound environment would add to the existing protections and further the international values represented by environmental law and human rights.

INTER-AMERICAN COMMISSION ON HUMAN RIGHTS

The Inter-American Commission on Human Rights has the authority to study the human rights situation generally or in regard to specific issues with a member state of the OAS.

The Commission in its discussion of relevant human rights law emphasized the Right to Life and physical security. It stated that:

> the realization of the Right to Life, and to physical security and integrity is necessarily related to and in some ways dependent upon one's physical environment. Accordingly, where environmental contamination and degradation pose a persistent threat to human life and health, the foregoing rights are implicated.[22]

In this regard, State Parties may be required to take positive measures to safeguard the fundamental and non-derogable rights to life and physical integrity, in particular to prevent the risk of severe environmental pollution that could threaten human life and health, or to respond when persons have suffered injury.

The Commission also directly addressed concerns for economic development, noting that the Convention neither prevent nor discourage it, but rather requires that it take place under conditions of respect for the rights of affected individuals. Thus, while the Right to Development implies that each State may exploit its natural resources, the absence of regulation, inappropriate regulation, or a lack of supervision in the application of extant norms may create serious problems with respect to the environment which translate into violations of human rights protected by the American Convention.[23]

The Commission concluded that conditions of severe environmental pollution, which may cause serious physical illness, impairment and suffering on the part of the local populace, are inconsistent with the right to be respected as a human being ...The quest to guard against environmental conditions which threaten human health requires that individuals have access to: information, participation in relevant decision-making processes, and judicial recourse.[24]

CONVENTION ON THE RIGHTS OF THE CHILD

The Convention on the Rights of the Child (New York, November 20, 1989) refers to aspects of environmental protection in respect to the child's right to health. Article 24 provides that States Parties shall take appropriate measures to combat disease and malnutrition "through the provision of adequate nutritious foods and clean drinking water, taking into consideration the dangers and risks of environmental pollution." (Art. 24(2)(c). Information and education is to be provided to all segments of society on hygiene and environmental sanitation. (Art. 24(2)(e).

In the context of the State reporting procedure, the

Committee on Rights of Child has issued observations calling for better compliance with Article 24(2)(c). In its Concluding Observations on the State report submitted by Jordan, the CRC recommended that Jordan "take all appropriate measures, including through international cooperation, to prevent and combat the damaging effects of environmental pollution and contamination of water supplies on children and to strengthen procedures for inspection."[25] The CRC's Concluding Observations on South Africa also expressed the Committee's "concern . . . at the increase in environmental degradation, especially as regards air pollution" and "recommended that the State Party increase its efforts to facilitate the implementation of sustainable development programmes to prevent environmental degradation, especially as regards air pollution."[26]

HUMAN RIGHTS COMMITTEE

The U.N. Human Rights Committee has indicated that state obligations to protect the Right to Life can include positive measures designed to reduce infant mortality and protect against malnutrition and epidemics.[27]

Cases involving the environment have been heard by the Human Rights Committee. Such as *EHP v. Canada,* implicated the Right to Life in an environmental context. In 1980, a resident of Port Hope, Ontario, alleged that large-scale dumping of nuclear waste had taken place within her community.[28] The dumpsites were closed, but approximately 200,000 tons of radioactive waste remained in Port Hope. The communication claimed that the wastes presented a threat to the life of "present and future generations" of Port Hope and a threat to health. Because the author of the communication had not yet exhausted domestic remedies, the communication was declared inadmissible.[29] However, in the process of dismissing the complaint, the Committee discussed the validity of the petitioner's environmental claims as matters of human rights concern and observed that the communication raised serious issues regarding the duty of State Parties to protect the Right to Life as provided by Article 6.1 of the International Covenant on Civil and Political Rights. This is an important finding because the Committee only reaches the question of exhaustion of local remedies after it had determined that the petitioner has a *prima facie* case concerning rights protected by the Covenant. One commentator has concluded based on this that environmental claims do fall within the ambit of the Covenant.

Another interesting aspect of the Port Hope case was the applicant's assertion that the rights of future generations had been violated by the dumping of nuclear wastes in the community. Needless to say, the rights of people not yet born are at issue in many cases involving the environment. The Committee left open the possibility that applicants can challenge violations to rights held by future generations. The Committee determined that the author had standing by virtue of her own situation, and therefore was not relying solely on the rights of future generations to sue. Thus, the Committee treated the author's reference to 'future generations' as an expression of concern purporting to put into due perspective the importance of the matter raised in the communication". Consequently, it is as yet unclear whether individuals may assert these rights. Nevertheless, this case suggests that environmental wrongs are appropriately addressed in human rights forums and that traditional notions of individual injury may warrant extension in case of environmental harm.

WORLD CONFERENCE ON HUMAN RIGHTS

The World Conference on Human Rights, held at Vienna from 14 to 25 June 1993, solemnly adopted the Vienna Declaration and Programme of Action containing 142 paragraphs on various aspects of human rights. It is worth quoting those directly related to the Right to Development and environment.

Part I, paragraphs 10 and 11 read as follows:

(Paragraph 10): The World Conference on Human Rights reaffirms the Right to Development, as established in the

Declaration on the Right to Development, as a universal and inalienable right and an integral part of fundamental human rights. As stated in the Declaration on the Right to Development, the human person is the central subject of development. While development facilitates the enjoyment of all human rights, the lack of development may not be invoked to justify the abridgement of internationally recognized human rights.

States should cooperate with each other in ensuring development and eliminating obstacles to development. The international community should promote an effective international cooperation for the realization of the Right to Development and the elimination of obstacles to development. Lasting progress towards the implementation of the Right to Development requires effective development policies at the national level, as well as equitable economic relations and favourable economic environment at the international level."

(Paragraph 11): The Right to Development should be fulfilled so as to meet equitably the developmental and environmental needs of present and future generations. The World Conference on Human Rights recognises that illicit dumping of toxic and dangerous substances and waste potentially constitutes a serious threat to the human rights to life and health of everyone.

Consequently the World Conference on Human Rights calls on all states to adopt and vigorously implement existing Conventions relating to the dumping of toxic and dangerous products and waste and to cooperate in the prevention of illicit dumping. Everyone has the right to enjoy the benefits of scientific progress and its applications. The World Conference notes that certain advances, notably in the biomedical and life sciences as well as in information technology, may have potentially adverse consequences for the integrity, dignity and human rights of the individual, and calls for international cooperation to ensure that human rights and dignity are fully respected in this area of universal concern".

COMMISSION ON SUSTAINABLE DEVELOPMENT

In accordance with the provisions on International Institutional Arrangements of Agenda 21 adopted by the United Nations Conference on Environment and Development, and pursuant to General Assembly Resolution 47/191 of December 1992, the Economic and Social Council established the Commission on Sustainable Development on 12 February 1993 (decision 1993/207).

As recommended by the General Assembly in Resolution 47/191, the programme of work of the Commission will be based on clusters "that would integrate in an effective manner related sectoral and cross-sectoral components of Agenda 21 in such a way as to allow the Commission to review the progress of the implementation of the entire Agenda 21 by 1997.

The work clusters recommended are the following :

a) Critical elements of sustainability (Agenda 21, Chapters 2-5);

b) Financial resources and mechanism (Agenda 21, Chapter 33);

c) Education, science, transfer of environmentally sound technologies, cooperation and capacity building (Agenda 21, Chapters 16, 34 - 37);

d) Decision-making structures (Agenda 21, Chapters 8, 38-40);

e) Roles of major groups (Agenda 21, Chapters 23-32);

f) Health, human settlements and fresh water (Agenda 21, Chapters 6, 7, 18 and 21);

g) Land, desertification, forests and biodiversity (Agenda 21, Chapters 10 - 15);

h) Atmosphere, oceans and all kinds of seas (Agenda 21, Chapters 9, 17);

i) Toxic chemicals and hazardous wastes (Agenda 12, Chapters 19, 20 and 22).

The Commission on Sustainable Development in its Fifth Session (7-25 April 1997) related to "Rio Declaration on Environment and Development : application and implementation reviews the progress of implementation of the Principle 1[30] in the following way.

a) Principle 1 emphasizes the conviction of States that human beings are at the centre of environment and development and reflects, thus, an anthropocentric approach. Principle 1 reflects the fundamental human right to a life with dignity. All other principles of Rio Declaration are construed so as to give effect to this principle. Principle 1 is also concerned with human health, an aspect elaborated in chapter 6 of Agenda 21, paragraph 1 of which states "health and development are intimately interconnected .... Agenda 21 must address the primary health needs of the world's population, since they are integral to the achievement of the goals of sustainable development and primary environmental case". Paragraph 6.40 states "the overall objective is to minimize hazards and maintain the environment to a degree that human health and safety is not impaired or endangered and yet encourage development to proceed".

b) The right to a healthy environment has been frequently referred to, though often in non-legally binding instruments, and is often explicitly guaranteed and proclaimed in human rights treaty law. Since 1992, principle 1 has been recognised in treaty law, sometimes with reference to specific sectors. Examples are Preamble's paragraph 1 of the Desertification Convention and the Fourth Lome Convention which states that "cooperation shall be directed towards development centres on man, the main protagonist and beneficiary of development".[31]

c) The Programme of Action of the International Conference on Population and Development contains 14 principles.here in after referred to as the 1994 Cairo Principles.[32] Principle

2 states: "Human beings are at the centre of concerns for sustainable development. They are entitled to a healthy and productive life in harmony with nature. People are the most important and valuable resources of any nation. Countries should ensure that all individuals are given the opportunity to make the most of their potential. They have an adequate standard of living for themselves and their families, including adequate food, clothing, water and sanitation."

d) The right to a healthy and productive life in harmony with nature is often found in Constitutions and/or basic (environmental laws, formulated as a general principle of national environmental legislation). Almost all Constitutions adopted or revised in the past 35 years address environmental concerns.[33] Constitutional provision in a great number of States explicitly enunciate a right to a healthy environment.[34] Correspondingly, almost all of the Constitutions provide both an obligation of the State to conserve and a duty of the citizens to protect, the environment, the constitutional obligation on the part of the State to conserve the environment corroborates the right to a healthy environment that is in some cases formulated in terms of an individual's right to a healthy environment.

e) The Supreme Court of the Philippines decided that while the right to a balanced and healthful ecology is to be found under the Declaration of Principles and State Policies and not under the Bill of Rights, it does not follow that it is less important than any of the civil and political rights enumerated in the latter. Such a right belongs to a different category of rights altogether, for it concerns nothing less than self-preservation and self-perpetuation [... ...] the advancement of which may even be said to predate all Governments and Constitutions. As a matter of fact, these basic rights need not even be written in the Constitution for they are assumed to exist from the inception of humankind.[35]

THE CONSTITUTION OF INDIA AND CLEAN ENVIRONMENT

Article 21 of the Constitution of India guarantees Right to Life. This negative right has been interpreted by the Supreme Court of India in two ways, one is that deprivation of personal liberty should be fair, just and reasonable[36], and another is that Supreme Court of India has recognized certain unarticulated liberties as implied from Right to Life.[37] It is by this Second method that Supreme Court of India has recognized Right to Life to include Right to Clean Environment.

The question whether Right to a Clean Environment is part of the Right to Life was examined by the Supreme Court in *Subhash Kumar v. State of Bihar.*[38] In this case Supreme Court declared that the right to a wholesome environment formed an integral part of the Right to Life guaranteed by Article 21 of the Indian Constitution.

The Court stated:

> "The Right to Life is a Fundamental Right under Article 21 of the Constitution and it includes the right of enjoyment of pollution-free water and air for full enjoyment of life. If anything endangers or impairs that quality of life in derogation of laws, a citizen has the right to have recourse to Article 32 of the Constitution for removing the pollution of water or air which may be detrimental to the quality of life."[39]

This role of the Court also finds support from the observations of Justice Singh in *Ganga Pollution Tanneries case*[40] as justifying its closure. The Court noted in conclusion: "we are conscious that closure of tanneries may bring unemployment, loss of revenue, but life, health and ecology have greater importance to the people". Besides, some High Courts have also accorded recognition to this environmental dimension of Article 21 such as judgement by the Andhra Pradesh High Court in *T. Damodar Rao v. Special Officer Municipal Corporation,*

Hyderabad[41] explicitly recognised an environmental dimension to Article 21 while considering a writ petition to enjoin the Life Insurance Corporation and Income Tax Department from building residential houses in a recreation zone, held : "It would be reasonable to hold that the enjoyment of life and its attainment and fulfillment guaranteed by Article 21 of the Constitution embraces the protection and preservation of nature's gifts without which life cannot be enjoyed. There can be no reason why practice of violent extinguishment of life alone should be regarded as violative of Article 21 of the Constitution. The slow poisoning by the polluted atmosphere caused by environmental pollution and spoliation should also be regarded as violative of Article 21 of the Constitution. The Court held that the attempt of the respondents to build houses in this area is contrary to law and also contrary to Article 21 of the Constitution".[42]

In the judgement of *Lakshmipathy v. State of Karnataka*[43] the Karnataka High Court made the following observations: "The movement for restoration and maintenance of a livable environment requires curbing of power of narrowly oriented administrative agencies in appropriation of the dwindling acreage of land and water not already irrevocably appropriate". "Environment Protection is not a pre-occupation of the educated and affluent. It has a socio-political dimension. The disposal and the control of toxic waste and governmental regulation of polluting industries is public interest oriented. The effective implementation of environmental legislation is a social learning process which could bring fundamental change in the character of public administration". "The Right to Life, inherent in Article 21 of the Constitution does not fall short of requirements of qualitative life which is possible only in an environment of quality. Where, on account of human agencies, the quality of air and the quality of environment are threatened or affected, the Court would not hesitate to use its innovative power within its jurisdiction to enforce and safeguard the Right to Life to promote public interest".

CONCLUSION

Important developments have occurred at the national and international levels. They indicate a growing inter-connectedness between the fields of human rights and environmental protection. The overall context for these developments is the concept of sustainable development, which requires that different societal objectives be treated in an integrated manner.

Many International Organizations and United Nations Agencies have also addressed the connection between human rights and the environment in their organizational structures and activities, particularly through the adoption of policies that favour access to environmental information and public participation in their procedures, but also through their policies aimed at sustainable development and poverty alleviation.

From a review of the decisions of International Treaty Bodies (including Courts and Commissions), a substantial body of case law and decisions has recognized the violation of a fundamental human right as the cause, or result, of environmental degradation. A significant number of decisions at the national and international levels have identified environmental harm to individuals or communities, arising as a result of violations of the rights to health, to life, to self-determination, to food and water, and to housing. Particularly in the European system, a clear connection has been made between a violation of the right to privacy and home life and the right not to be subject to pollution, including the right to know whether pollution is likely to affect a particular individual or community.

We must acknowledge that 'Right to Life' is not absolute too. If the State guarantees to its citizens the security of life, the citizens must owe a duty to State to maintain its sanctity. Man has not to simply live, but to live well and living well means a living moral, virtuous and healthy and happy life. My right of living involves my duty to my fellow-men to allow them the same condition of life. Happiness and prosperity in a society is an *onto* function. I can enjoy my rights only if I respect the rights of others. Man cannot lead a life of isolation. Dependence is his very psychology and individuals depend on one another and on the State as a whole.

So from the foregoing discussion we can say that "human life would be nowhere if the sacredness of this claim is not accepted. The Right to Life is, therefore, the most fundamental of all rights, as it is the very core of humanity. It means a claim to so live that the existence does not jeopardise the existence of others". The protection of the Right to Life should be examined globally, taking into consideration the context of various societies, as well as the need for the protection of the full dignity of human being in its different philosophical and ideological meanings. Among others it is indispensable to demonstrate the scope of protection in its various extensions: in terms, in stages, and in intensity.

REFERENCES

1. United Nations General Assembly (UNGA) (xxii), 3 December 1968.
2. Declaration of the United Nations on the Human Environment (1972) 11 ILM 1416, Preamble and Principle 1.
3. Declaration of the Hague (1989) 28 ILM 1308, Preamble.
4. UNGA Resolution 45/94, 14 December 1990.
5. Resolution 1990/41, 6 March, 1990.
6. Draft Earth Charter, 26 August 1991; H. Hofmann (ed.), *Basic Documents of International Environment Law*, 1992, Vol. 3, p. 1748.
7. Rio Principle 3 : "The Right to Development must be fulfilled as to equitably meet developmental and environmental needs of present and future generations".
8. OECD, Responsibility and Liability of States in Relation to Transfrontier Pollution, 13 Environmental Policies and

Law (1984), p. 122.

9. Draft UNECE Charter on Environmental Rights and Obligations, adopted 29-31, 1990, quoted in D. Shelton, "Human Rights, Environmental Rights, and the Right to Environment", 28 *Stanford Journal of International Law* (Stanford California), (1991), Vol. 103, at fn. 84.

10. E. Brown Weirs in Fairness to Future Generations: International Law, Common Patrimony, and Intergenerational Equity, Tokyo 1989, Appendix B. See also Human Rights and Environment, Second Progress Report, UN Doc. E/CN.4/1993/7; the Special Rapporteur conducted an extensive study of national constitutions and jurisprudence.

11. UN Doc. E/CN.4/4. Sub. 2/1994/9.

12. A. Kiss and D. Shelton, *International Environmental Law*, Transnational Publications, 1991, p. 27.

13. Article 225 of Chapter VI.

14. *Lopez-Ostra v. Spain*, ECHR (1994), Series A, No. 303C.

15. Case 14967/89, *Guerra and Others v. Italy*, 1998-1 ECHR, Judgment of 19 February 1998.

16. EEC Directive on the Major Accident Hazards of Certain Industrial Activities, 82/501/EEC, 1982 O.J. 230, amended by 87/216/EEC, 19 March 1987. The Seveso law required disclosure of the production process; the substances present and their quantities; possible risks for employees, workers, the population and the environment; security measures, and rules to follow in case of accident. Other laws supplemented the right to environmental information.

17. The European Commission on Human Rights ceased to function with the entry into force of Protocol 11 to the European Convention which created a permanent European Court of Human Rights. Protocol No. 11 to the European Convention for the Protection of Human Rights and Fundamental Freedoms, adopted May 11, 1994, entered

into force Nov. 1, 1998, E.T.S. 155, *reprinted in* 33 I.L.M. 960 (1994). The new Court was inaugurated on Nov. 1, 1998.

18. *Guerra and Others v. Italy*, 1998-I ECHR, Judgment of 19 February 1998, para. 53.
19. *Ibid.* para. 60.
20. *Zimmerman and Steiner v. Switzerland*, ECHR (1983), Series A, No. 66.
21. *Pine Valley Development v. Ireland*, ECHR Ser. A No. 222 (1991). The Court did find a violation of Article 14 taken in conjunction with the right to peaceful enjoyment of possessions.
22. Inter-Am.C.H.R., *Report on the Situation of Human Rights in Ecuador*, OEA/Ser.L/V/II.96, doc. 10 rev. 1 (1997). at 88.
23. *Ibid.* at 89.
24. *Ibid.* at 92, 93.
25. U.N. Committee on the Rights of the Child, Concluding Observations on Jordan, U.N. Doc. CRC/C/15/Add.125 at para. 50 (2000).
26. U.N. Committee on the Rights of the Child, Concluding Observations on South Africa, U.N. Doc. CRC/C/15/Add.122 (200) at para. 30. *See also* Concluding Observations on Kyrgyzstan, U.N. Doc. CRC/C/15/Add. 127 (2000); Concluding Observations on Grenada, U.N. Doc. CRC/15/Add.121 (2000).
27. See the General Comment on Article 6 of the Civil and Political Covenant, issued by the United Nations Human Rights Committee, in *Compilation of General Comments and General Recommendations adopted by Human Rights Treaty Bodies*, U.N. Doc. HRI/GEN/1/Rev.3 (1997) 6-7 [hereinafter *Compilation*]
28. Communication No. 67/1980 (27 October 1982,

Seventeenth Session) reprinted in Selected Decision of the Human Rights Committee, Vol. 2 (October 1982 - April 1998) (United Nations Publication, Sales No. E.89.XIV.1), p. 20.

29. The application was declared inadmissible despite arguments by the author that domestic remedies would prove inadequate because of the difficulty of proving present injury, the possibility of protracted litigation and the inability under Canadian law to defend future generations. *Ibid.*, pp. 20-21.

30. Human beings are at the centre of concerns for sustainable development. They are entitled to a healthy and productive life in harmony with nature.

31. As revised by the Agreement signed in Mauritius on 4 November 1995. See The APC-EU Courier, No. 155 (January-February 1996).

32. A/CONF. 171/13/Rev. 1, Resolution 1, Annex, Chap. II.

33. E/CN.4/Sub.2/1994/9 of 6 July 1994.

34. Recent examples are the Constitution of Ukraine, adopted 28 June 1996; Constitution of South Africa, adopted 8 May 1996; Constitution of Ethopia, adopted 8 December 1994; Constitution of Argentina, adopted 23 August 1994.

35. Supreme Court of the Philippines, Manila, 30 July 1993, Minors Oposa V. Secretary of the Department of Environment and Natural Resources, G.R. No. 101083, reprinted in 33 ILM 173, 187 (1994).

36. *Maneka Gandhi's Case* , AIR 1978, SC 597.

37. *Khark Singh v. State of U.P.*, AIR 1963, SC1295., *Francis Coralie Mullin v. The Administrator of Delhi*, AIR 1981, SC 746.

38. *Subhash Kumar v. State of Bihar*, AIR, 1991, SC 420.

39. *Ibid.*

40. *M.C. Mehta v. Union of India*, AIR 1988 SC 1037.

41. AIR, 1987 AP 171.

42. *Rural Litigation and Entitlement Kendra, Dehradun v. State Uttar Pradesh*, AIR, 1985, SC 652, AIR 1988 SC 2187.

43. AIR, 1992 Karnataka 57.

4

Environmental Pollution and Its Impact on Health

The environment has been defined as that outer physical and biological system in which man and other organisms live as a whole. This entire system is a complicated one as it has many interacting components. These components of the environment generally include : "its rocks, minerals, soils, waters, its land and their present and potential vegetation, its animal life and potential for livestock husbandry, and its climate".[1] There is a close and complicated interaction among these various components which tend to produce some kind of equilibrium in the scheme of nature what is usually termed as 'ecological balance.' Changes in the ecological system occur continuously through natural process and man's activities but the system to a certain extent has a remarkable tendency to rebalance itself. This system as a whole is useful to man. Perhaps it is due to this usefulness that for fulfilling his physical requirement, man is totally dependent on environment.[2] But with the passage of time industrialization of society, the introduction of motorised vehicles, and the explosion of human population, however have caused an exponential growth in the production of goods and services, coupled with this growth there has been a tremendous increase in waste by-products. The indiscriminate discharge of untreated industrial wastes containing most insidious and persistent toxic pollutants into waterways, the spewing of thousands of tons of particulates and air-borne gases into atmosphere, indiscriminate use of non-biodegradable materials, throw-away attitude towards solid wastes, in brief man's instinct of selfishness, profit-oriented motto led him towards indiscriminate exploitation of natural wealth, in this way imbalanced the nature's capacity of self-stabilization. Discharge of effluents into atmosphere, ozone layer depletion, global warming, droughts and floods, oil spills, acid rains, dumping or refuge are unpleasant ramifications of growing environmental pollution which has posed many problems world over.

Today man has made a remarkable progress in various fields of science and technology. This would not have been possible had he not exploited natural resources. Science has given us all the material comforts which we could not have dreamt of some decades ago. To meet the increasing needs of burgeoning population, every effort is being made by scientists and technologists to produce more goods and services with the help of latest technology., But what has been the effect of all this on our environment ? A global disaster.[3]

Environmental crises are closely linked with the nature of modern technology such as generation of synthetic and non-biodegradable substances in the form of plastics, chemical nitrogen fertilizers, synthetic detergents, synthetic fibers, petrochemicals and other environmentally injurious industries and 'disposable culture'.[4]

We, humans are, as Virginia W. Rasumussen puts it, technological creatures and 'tinkering is our nature'.[5] Tinkering with nature is, unfortunately, not always done intelligently enough to avoid its impairment. People are not aware, or not aware enough, of the consequences of the ecologically unsound activities. Many such activities, and primarily those linked to the improper use of science and technology are going on in the world, causing deforestation, desertification, pollution of air, water and land, damage to many plant and animal species and threats to other renewable as well as non-renewable resources of our planet. Although we have ecologically benign technologies but they are not utilized because they are considered inconsistent with short-term interests of private profit maximization.[6] Such as in case of developing countries development is sometimes taken as a priority and an excuse for the massive impairment of the environment voluntarily or involuntarily. Many mistakes are made including some of those already made by the developed countries long ago. Weak economies, unstable political system, military adventures, non-existent or bad environment policies, unfavourable climate, the population explosion, and many other factors only make the situation worse.

The developed countries, instead of increasing their efforts to help the developing countries in all possible ways to overcome their hardships and to make our world a better place for all, are often more interested in their own short-term interests. While giving some aid and financial assistance directly or through International Organizations, they allow their firms, and especially some multinational corporations, to use the labour and natural resources of the third world without taking adequate measures for environmental protection. The work of the corporations, at least some of them, often impairs the environment even in the industrialized countries themselves. Their activities could be, as Capra wrote, "altogether disastrous in the third world. In those countries, where legal restrictions are often non-existent or impossible to enforce, the exploitation of people and of their land has reached extreme proportions".[7]

It has been repeatedly stressed in many important international documents[8], conferences and other fora, and by distinguished experts, that major changes in international economic and other closely interrelated domains are needed. The World Commission on Environment and Development believes, for instance, that: "Two conditions must be satisfied before international economic exchanges can become beneficial for all involved. The sustainability of the ecosystem on which global economy depends must be guaranteed. And the economic partners must be satisfied that the basis of exchange is equitable, relationships that are unequal and based on dominance of one kind or another are not a sound durable basis for interdependence.

For many developing countries neither condition is met".[9] Both of the conditions should constitute basic elements of any new international economic order[10] or any other serious attempt to change international economic relations in general so as to better and improve the position of developing countries in particular. Keeping in view the importance of the ecological issue as a basic pre-requisite for both the improvement of the economic situation in the world which is guarantee for better protection and promotion of human rights.

POLLUTION AND ITS IMPACT ON HEALTH

A man with a poor health is a liability to the community he lives in. And a community burdened with ill-health is an impoverished community because ill-health and poverty often go together. The vicious circle of disease — low production, low income, poor health services, more diseases, and more poverty - not only poses a problem of health and sanitation but also of social welfare and social justice. It invariably creates hopelessness, dejection, lethargy and disrespect for law and the moral code of conduct.[11]

A peasant sick at a critical period of planting and harvesting cannot produce enough to feed himself and his family. An industrial worker unable to attend to his work regularly cannot augment his income to the extent it is necessary to lead a comfortable life. A child unable to attend school cannot equip itself with the knowledge and training necessary for good living. It is not only the question of few individuals suffering from certain diseases, the cumulative impact of poor health on man's life is more far-reaching than we ordinarily realise. It was for this reason that the WHO defined health as "a state of complete physical, mental and social well-being and not merely the absence of disease and infirmity".[12]

Human diseases can be said to be the net result of the "convergence in time and space, within the person, or the patient, of environment stimuli, organic or inorganic. These stimuli are a challenge which induce a tissular response, that is, disease (communicable, degenerative or behavioural) which in turn eventually results in ecologic adaptation and survival or in total maladjustment and death".[13] Disease is thus "that alteration of the living tissues which jeopardises survival in their environment and which results from an accidental collision between two or more forms of life, each pursuing its own destiny".[14]

The two forms of life which collide with each other to create human diseases are human beings and minute organisms like bacteria, viruses. These organisms, after entering the body of man, function in an environment which is determined by heredity and external stresses. Before entering the human body they have to breed, survive and grow in a different set of environmental conditions. The organism will succeed in jeopardising the health of a person only when both the external environment (geographical and socio-cultural) in which it originates and internal environment (the human body) in which it grows offer favourable conditions for multiplication.

It's not just the lung that serves as a gateway for hazardous pollutants, but it's also the gastro-intestinal tract. It's not just lung cancer, but also bladder cancer that is related to smoking. Lead may be inhaled through the lung, but it has its effect on bone, blood, and the central nervous system. Carbon monoxide, too, gains access into the body by the lung, but has its greatest effect on cardiovascular system".[15]

AIR POLLUTION

According to World Health Organisation, "air pollution can be described as substances put into air by activity of mankind into concentrations sufficient to cause harmful effects to health, property, crop yield or to interfere with the enjoyment of property".[16]

Main Sources of Air Pollution

(a) The combustion of fuels to produce energy for heating and power.

(b) Transportation

(c) Industrial and commercial processes.

(d) Incineration.

Effects of Air Pollution

Every day a person inhales about 7500 litres of air so that his lungs and respiratory system have been in contact with.[17] As during the process of combustion of fossil fuels, many oxides of carbon and particulates are generated. Apart from this, various industries generate pollutants, like Sulphur dioxide (SO_2), Nitrogen dioxide (NO_2), ammonia, hydrocarbons and other toxic substances including lead, fluorides etc. The vehicles which use leaded fuel account for about 95 per cent of air-borne lead pollution[18] which may result in loss of intelligence quotient (IQ) and increase in crime levels. Particulate pollution, either on its own or in combination with Sulphur dioxide, leads to wide range of respiratory and exacerbating heart diseases, causing at least 500,000 premature deaths and 4-5 million new cases of chronic bronchitis each year (World Bank 1992). As per World Bank study 1995, ambient air pollution levels (particles less than 10 microns in diameter (PM 10)*, Sulphur dioxide, lead and nitrogen oxides) exceeding World Health Organization standards in 36 major Indian cities/towns account for 40,350 premature deaths, 1,98,500 thousand hospital admissions and sickness requiring medical treatment, and 1210 million incidences of minor sickness annually.

---

* Particulate Matter is a complex mixture of very tiny solid or liquid particles, composed of chemicals, soot, and dust. Because of only very small particles can be inhaled into lungs, health standards for the quality of ambient air are based on mass concentration of "inhalable particles", defined to include microscopic, invisible particles that are 10 microns (millions of a metre) or less in diameter called PM 10. The smallest of these inhalable particles, those 205 microns and smaller, are called PM 2.5.

AIR POLLUTION AND WOMEN'S HEALTH

Many chemical pollutants have the potential to produce estrogenic effects when absorbed into the body, and may be a factor in breast cancer development. Organochlorines such as DDT, PCBs, and polycyclic aromatic hydrocarbons (PAH) petroleum by-products have been shown in animal studies to mimic estrogen, and may have induced or promoted mammary tumors in rats. These chemicals can be inhaled as air pollutants resulting from industrial manufacturing, energy production, and traffic exhaust. Many of these toxins are stored in fat and may reside in the body for long periods of time. Storage of toxins in fat is a problem of greater importance in women because of their higher percent of body fat and the hormonal changes that occur during pregnancy, lactation, and menopause, which can result in mobilizing internal stores of pollutants many years after the initial exposure. Exposure to occupational chemicals may affect reproductive capacity adversely in the form of reduced fertility, spontaneous abortion, low birth weight, birth defects and developmental disabilities.[19]

AIR POLLUTION AND CHILDREN'S HEALTH

Children are more vulnerable to air-borne pollution for many reasons, including the fact that their airways are narrower than adults, they have markedly increased needs for oxygen relative to their size, they breathe more rapidly and inhale more pollutants per pound of body weight, and they spend more time engaged in vigorous outdoor activities than adults. Existing epidemiologic studies indicate a relationship between outdoor air pollution and adverse respiratory effects in children, and the most common pollutants implicated are respirable particulates and ozone. Air pollution correlates with increased prevalence of chronic cough, chest illness, bronchitis, hospital admissions for respiratory conditions, and decrements in lung function.[20]

AIR POLLUTION AND AGED PEOPLE

Senior citizens have been identified as a population at

special risk with regard to environmental pollution. Senior citizens have the advantage of long-range perspective than most citizens and have accumulated considerable wisdom. However, their age puts them at a disadvantage in terms of health because of environmental pollution hazards' cumulative nature. Aging individuals are more susceptible to air pollution because of the declining margin of safety in various organ systems, including the respiratory and immune systems, and because, in some cases, of the cumulative effect of environmental hazards. Seniors, along with children, are most at risk in severe air pollution episodes. Skin cancer and other malignancies are much more prevalent among the elderly, like the cumulative effect of sun exposure over time expressing itself. The elderly are also affected by environmental pollution in other ways, for example, there is concern about their emotional health related to the environment, especially if they live in areas with serious air pollution problems, which may cause stress, anxiety and depression in addition to physical problems.[21]

Besides many health problems, air pollution impacts economic productivity, especially agricultural productivity; damages material property such as buildings and land; and causes ecological changes that increase risks of environmental disasters. Emissions of Sulphur dioxide and Nitrogen oxides lead to deposition of acid rain and other acidic compounds over long distances often more than 1,000 kilometers from their source. Acid deposition changes the chemical balance of soils and can lead to the leaching of trace minerals and nutrients critical to trees and plants. The links between forest damage and acid deposition are complex. Direct exposure to high levels of Sulphur dioxide or acid deposition can cause defoliation and dieback.[22] Carbon dioxide (CO_2) emissions, largely a by-product of energy production and use, account for the largest sharc of green house gases, which are associated with global warming. Scientists believe that global warming may be responsible for important changes in the world's climate and environment such as altered patterns of rainfall, droughts and melting of polar glaciers.

WATER POLLUTION

Water pollution means such alteration of the physical, chemical or biological properties of water, or, discharge of any sewage or industrial waste, or of any other substance liquid or gaseous, into water, which may or is likely to render such water harmful or injurious to public health or safety, or to domestic, commercial, industrial, agriculture or other legitimate uses, or to the life and health of animals or plants or of aquatic organisms.

It is a well-known fact that clean water is absolutely essential for healthy living. Adequate supply of fresh water and clean drinking water is a basic need for all human beings on the earth. Water pollution has become one of the greatest problem in context of environmental pollution in general. The problem generates specific concern in view of the scarce availability of usable water and ever increasing demands as the quality of available freshwater resources all over the world are threatened not only by over exploitation and poor management but also by ecological degradation.

SOURCE OF WATER POLLUTION

The major sources of water pollution are domestic waste water, emission of organic pollutants from industrial activities and agricultural run off. Polluting substances include organic matter, metals, minerals, sediments, toxic chemicals etc.

EFFECTS OF WATER POLLUTION

Any chemical can become a pollutant in water causing one or more of these effects if it is present in high concentrations, example is that of organic pollutants containing bio-degradable organic chemicals which generally act as pollutants in the sense that they contain chemicals that provide food for micro-organisms which multiply rapidly as a result of the increased food input. The micro-organisms in the process of growing and oxidizing the organic chemical food stuff, use up the dissolved oxygen rapidly which in some cases lead to death of higher organisms, like fish.[23]

Despite critical parameters affecting water quality such as high biochemical oxygen demand[24] and total coliform, domestic and human waste is the cause of many water-borne diseases such as diarrhoea, hepatitis (jaundice), hookworm infection, trachoma, and dracunculiasis (guinea worm). Due to inadequate sewage disposal facilities, refuse invariably gets mixed with open waste water resources, leading to water-borne diseases, and health hazards such as malaria, filariasis, and even epidemics such as cholera, can spread. Recent World Bank and World Health Organization data shows that about 21 percent of all communicable diseases in India (11.5 per cent of all diseases) are water related.[25]

Many of our rivers and lakes are getting contaminated from industrial effluents and agricultural run-off with toxic chemicals and heavy metals (such as mercury, chromium, lead and arsenic) which are hard to remove from drinking water with standard purification facilities, in this way making it unfit for human consumption. The other main concern is the ground water pollution due to leaching from surface source like agricultural field and waste dumps. The depths of the water table at which tube wells draw water are increasing and as a result inorganic pollutants such as arsenic and fluoride are leached out leading to chronic health hazards like arsenic poisoning and fluorosis, as happened in West Bengal and Bangladesh.[26]

Ground water can be contaminated in many different ways, some of the most common reasons are listed below :

Pesticides: Run-off from farms, backyards, and golf courses contain pesticides such as DDT that in turn contaminate the water. Leachate from landfill sites is another major contaminating source. Its effects on the ecosystems and health are endocrine and reproductive damage in wildlife. Groundwater is susceptible to contamination, as pesticides are mobile in the soil. It is a matter of concern as these chemicals are persistent in soil and water.[27]

Sewage: Untreated or inadequately treated municipal sewage is a major source of groundwater and surface water pollution. The organic material that is discharged with municipal waste into water courses uses substantial oxygen for biological degradation thereby upsetting the ecological balance of rivers and lakes. Sewage also carries microbial pathogens that are the cause of the spread of disease.[28]

Nutrients: Domestic waste water, agricultural run off, and industrial effluents contain phosphorus and nitrogen, fertilizer run off, measure from livestock operations, which increase the level of nutrients in water bodies and can cause eutrophication in the lakes and rivers and continue on to the coastal areas. The nitrates come mainly from fertilizers that is added to the fields. Excessive use of fertilizers causes nitrate contamination of groundwater, with the result that nitrate levels in drinking water are far above the safety levels recommended. Good agricultural practices can help in reducing the amount of nitrates in the soil and thereby lower its content in the water.[29]

Synthetic organics: Many of the 100,000 synthetic compounds in use today are found in the aquatic environment and accumulate in the food chain. POPs or Persistent Organic Pollutant, represent the most harmful element for the ecosystem and for human health, for example, industrial chemicals and agricultural pesticides. These chemicals can accumulate in fish and cause serious damage to human health. Where pesticides are used on a large-scale, ground water gets contaminated and this leads to the chemical contamination of drinking water.[30]

A large number of chemicals that either exist naturally in the land or added due to human activity dissolve in the water, thereby contaminating it and leading to various diseases.

Pesticides: The organophosphates and the carbonates present in pesticides affect and damage the nervous system and can cause cancer. Some of the pesticides contain carcinogens that exceed recommended levels. They contain chlorides that cause reproductive and endocrinal damage.[31]

Lead: Lead is hazardous to health as it accumulates in the body and affects the central nervous system. Children and pregnant women are most at risk.[32]

Fluorides : Excess fluorides can cause yellowing of the teeth and damage to the spinal cord and other crippling diseases.[33]

Nitrates: Drinking water that gets contaminated with nitrates can prove fatal especially to infants that drink formula milk as it restricts the amount of oxygen that reaches the brain causing the 'blue baby' syndrome. It is also linked to digestive tract cancers. It causes algae to bloom resulting in eutrophication in surface water.[34]

Petrochemicals: Benzene and other petrochemicals can cause cancer even at low exposure levels.[35]

Chlorinated solvents: These are linked to reproduction disorders and to some cancers.[36]

Arsenic: Arsenic poisoning through water can cause liver and nervous system damage, vascular diseases and also skin cancer.[37]

Other Heavy metals: Heavy metals cause damage to the nervous system and the kidney, and other metabolic disruptions.[38]

LAND POLLUTION

Land pollution may be regarded as despoilation of urban and rural scene, disruption of natural landscape surface by any human activity, detection of land or chemical contamination of land. With the changing standards about the very conception of pollution, an objective definition of land pollution is any physical or chemical alteration to land which causes its use to change and render it incapable of beneficial use without treatment.

Presently the solid wastes in the form of non-biodegradable substances like plastics and other synthetic materials are biggest threat to arable land, coupled with this problem the efforts by people to increase agricultural productivity through the excessive use of chemical fertilizers, and pesticides have insidious health impacts. The excessive use of chemical fertilizers can alter the chemistry of soil and pesticide poisoning is common in developing countries.[39]

SOLID WASTES

Solid wastes such as biodegradable and non-biodegradable substances when not collected and disposed off efficiently and effectively, attracts rodents and flies which then spread diseases. It also pollutes and degrades land and water resources. If these wastes are left untreated, they would ferment slowly and would produce biogas which would be discharged into atmosphere. The bio-gas contains 65-75 percent methane gas which is a greenhouse gas having global warming potential 34 times more than that of carbon dioxide.[40]

The hospital refuse which consists of disposable needles knives, diapers, cotton examination govens, transfusion fittings, bed pads and so forth is highly infectious waste. The careless discarding of hypodermic needles after use into waste baskets has unfortunately frequently resulted in janitors becoming infected when they employ their hands to clean out the residue from waste containers. Simultaneously the hospital refuse contains high concentration of pathogenic bacteria which according to Armstrong[41] were found to be potential transmitters of air-borne bacteria.

NOISE POLLUTION

Noise means unwanted and undesired sound. Thus otherwise sound and noise can be taken to mean the same thing, but in considering our acoustic environment we must differentiate between these two terms. It is only when the effects of a sound are undesirable, it may be termed as noise.[42] The presence of noise in the open atmosphere or in confined space is generally considered undesirable, except possibly by the person responsible for it. This is termed as noise pollution. In the latter case noise pollution does not exist in the space immediately surrounding the person.[43]

Thus when the loudness of the sound is irritating or unbearable we regard it as noise pollution. A decibel (DB) is the standard unit for the measurement of noise. The zero on a decibel scale is at the threshold of hearing, the lowest sound pressure that can be heard. On this scale, according to Smith, the noted industrial psychologist of the 20th century, 20 DB is whisper, 40 DB, the noise in quiet office, 60 DB is normal conversation, 80 in Bus, 100 in train and 140 DB is the level at which sound becomes physically painful.[44]

SOURCES OF NOISE POLLUTION

The main sources of noise pollution are:

(i) Industry,

(ii) Construction work,

(iii) Traffic noise including engine and horn,

(iv) Power saws,

(v) Aircraft noise,

(vi) Radio, T.V. and Loudspeakers,

(vii) Demolition sites,

(viii) Fire crackers,

(ix) Surface Transport

EFFECTS OF NOISE POLLUTION

The effects of noise pollution on human mechanism could be broadly as follows.

(a) Physiological,

(b) Psychological and Behavioural effects.

(a) Physiological Effects:

The researchers of noise say that noise level in excess of 90 decibels for continuous periods can cause loss of hearing. A single exposure of 150 decibels is known to cause permanent injury to the internal mechanism of the ear.[45]

Prolonged chronic noises can also produce stomach ulcers as it may slow the process of secretion of gastric juice and change its acidity. It may lead to abortions and other congenital defects in unborn children.[46]

Some empirical research conducted on animals (especially on pregnant female mice) reveals that aircrafts taking off which brings in 120 to 150 decibels caused miscarriages in them. Similarly, high noise is capable to create these disturbances in human beings also. An analysis of more than 2,25,000 births in Los Angeles area by Dr. Norwell Jones[47], showed that there were more birth defects among babies whose mothers lived near the international airport than those who lived in quieter sections.

(b) Psychological and Behavioural Effects:

Noise is recognised as a major factor causing tension in the modern age. The psychological and behavioural effects created by excessive noise include annoyance, speech interference, fatigue, psychosomatic disorders, tension related diseases, sleep interference, mental illness and emotional distress. Loss of concentration and memory are also other inevitable consequences of noise pollution. According to Survey of Society for Clean Environment (SOCLEEN) 36 percent of the population in the Bombay city constantly encountered noise pollution. Of them 76 percent felt lack of concentration, 69 per cent complained disturbed sleep and 65 percent restlessness.[48]

CONCLUSION

The environmental pollution is silent attacker which directly or indirectly is responsible for health hazards, sickness and other ailments and loss of income due to reduced work and has added to the woes of human beings. Environmental degradation has become a major cause of worry for future generations. There is a substantial and growing base of biophysical indicators to inform decision-makers, analysts and the public about the state of the natural environment and the range of human activities that place pressures on human environment. 'Shri Gus Speth' the former Chairman of the Council of Environmental Quality (America) has rightly warned that due to our limited knowledge of the earth working, we should not experiment with its great system in a way that imposes unknown and potentially large risks on future generations.[49]

Our father of nation Gandhijee has clearly stated that "Nature produces enough for our wants if everybody took enough for himself and nothing more; there would be no pauperism and starvation in this world".[50] In line with Gandhian ideals Prof. Galbreith raises voice against the growth of multinational corportions (MNCs) which are concerned not with the consumers' well-being of present and future but their own.[51] He strongly recommends for other goals so that new industrial state would become responsive to the larger purpose of society.[52] These goals would be essentially moral, human and ecologically balancing.

REFERENCES

1. The State of World Environment, United Nations Environment Programme : Annual Review (1980), p. 6.
2. Virendra Kumar, '*Environmental Protection and Law*' in Paras Diwan (ed.), Environment Protection 1987, p. 81.
3. B.K. Sharma, H. Kaur, *An Introduction to Environmental Pollution*, Meerut, Goel Publishing House, 1997, Preface.
4. Commoner, *Making Peace with Planet* (New York : Pantheon, 1990), pp 46-47.
5. As cited by Vid Vukasovic, "Human Rights and Environmental Issues" in *Human Rights and Scientific and Technological Development*, C.G. Weeramentry, Tokyo, United Nations University Press, 1990, p. 185.
6. Commoner, *Op.cit.*, p. 101.

7. Fritjof Capra, *The Turning Point : Scientific Society and the Rising Culture* (Frontana, London, 1984), p. 234.

8. The UN Declaration on the Right to Development (GA Res 41/128); The World Charter for Nature (GA Res 3201-2/S-IV); The Charter of Economic Rights and Duties of States (GA, Res. 32/XXIX), etc.

9. World Commission on Environment and Development, Our Common Future (Oxford University Press, 1987), Annex. 1.

10. As cited by Vid Vukasovic, *Op.cit.*, p. 194.

11. U.N.O., Dept. of Social Affairs : Preliminary Report on the World Social Situation with Reference to Standard of Living, New York, 1952, p. 180 (1952 IV. 11).

12. WHO : Constitution of the WHO, Geneva, 1964, p. 3.

13. R.P. Misra, *Medical Geography of India*, New Delhi, National Book Trust India, 1970, p. 31.

14. *Ibid.*

15. http://www.nutramed.com/environment/airpollutionintro.htm

16. http://www.who.int/environmental_information/Air/Guidelines/Introduction.htm

17. G.R. Chhatwal and Others, *Encyclpaedia of Environmental Pollution and its Control*, Vol. I, New Delhi, Anmol Publications, 1989, p. 214.

18. "World Resources, 1996-97", As cited by Kirit S. Parikh and Others in *India Development Report 1997*, Delhi, Oxford University Press, p. 96.

19. *Supra note* 15.

20. *Ibid.*

21. *Ibid.*

22. *World Development Indicators 1999*, The World Bank, Washington DC, USA, p. 168.

23. Roy M. Harrison, *Pollution, Causes, Effects and Control*, Royal Society of Chemistry, Cambridge, 2001, p. 2.
24. Biochemical Oxygen Demand (BOD) measures the strength of an organic waste in terms of the amount of oxygen consumed by bacteria in breaking down waste.
25. *World Development Report*, 1993, pp. 216-219.
26. Kirit S. Parikh, *India Development Report*, 1999-2000, Delhi, Oxford University Press, p. 88.
27. http://edugreen.teri.res.in/explore/water/health.htm
28. *Ibid.*
29. *Ibid.*
30. *Ibid.*
31. *Ibid.*
32. *Ibid.*
33. *Ibid.*
34. *Ibid.*
35. *Ibid.*
36. *Ibid.*
37. *Ibid.*
38. *Ibid.*
39. World Development Indicators 1999, *Op.cit.*, p. 127.
40. Kirit S. Parikh and Others, "Environment can Neglect No Longer", *India Development Report 1997*, Delhi, Oxford University Press, p. 101.
41. G.R. Chhatwal and Others, *Encyclopedia of Environmental Pollution and Its Control*, Vol. iv, New Delhi, Anmol Publications, 1989, p. 36.
42. *Encyclopedia of Britannica*, Vol. 16, 1968, p. 558.
43. Professor Chandra Pal, "Environmental Pollution and Development, Environmental Law, Policy and Role of Judiciary. Mittal Publications, New Delhi, 1999, p. 177.

44. *Ibid.*, p. 178.
45. *Ibid.*
46. D.K. Dixit, "Noise Pollution", *Mirror*, Sept. 1984, p. 96.
47. Dr. Norwell Jones is a Professor of Psychology at the University of California, See also Bruce L. Welch and Annemarie (ed.) Physiological Effects of Noise, New York, 1970, p. 152.
48. *Indian Express*, Chandigarh, June 16, 1987, p. 6.
49. As cited by Pashpati N. Singh in '*Environment and Economic Development*', (N. Rajalakshmi), Delhi, Manak Publishers, 2000, p. 77.
50. Mahatma Gandhi, *Servodaya*, pp. 13,14.
51. N. Rajalakshmi, *Op.cit.*, p. 78.
52. Shriman Narayan, *Relevance of Gandhian Economics*, 1970, p. 218.

5

Environmental Challenges of Urbanization

Urbanization is the spatial dimension of industrial and technological revolution or economic and social development in general.[1]

The terminology involved in such a study and the interrelationship between its constituents needs to be understood first, which will help in understanding the nature, role and functions of the urban areas and the process of urbanization. By the term 'Urbanization' what is usually understood is the increasing proportion of total population living in urban areas (or settlements defined as 'urban' by census department on certain criteria). This demographic conception of urbanization, however, is transcended by many other uses of the term in which urbanization is recognized as a social process which has brought about great transformations in man's way of life. For the purpose of convenience, especially in statistical studies. 'Urban' and 'Urbanization' are usually considered merely in demographic sense, as agglomerations of a given size or as the proportion of total population living in places of a given size.[2] Sociologically, however, another meaning is understood, which is the 'spread of urbanism' or 'urban way of life' of the people (one could be urban, even if he is physically residing in a village).

In economic terms it is the increasing proportion of the people depending on non-agricultural activities - on the urban sector of the occupational pattern (secondary or manufacturing, and tertiary or trade, commerce and other services).

The 'United Nations' report on the social situation (1957) describes 'Urbanization' as the process whereby an increasing proportion of a country's population lives in the urban localities. The degree of urbanization - the extent to which a country is urbanized will be understood to mean the percentage of its population living in urban localities as of a given data. Urbanization implies profound social and cultural change for those involved in it, particularly in the less developed regions where the gulf is vast between the life in a large modern city and life in a village with traditional living patterns (sometimes estimated to be equivalent to hundreds, or even thousands of years of historical development).

While the term "urban area" is typically used as a synonym for "city", the two are not same. All cities are urban areas, but not all urban areas are cities. "Urban" is a statistical concept defined by a country's government. A city, on the other hand, is more than just large number of people living in close proximity to one another; it is a complex political, economic, and social entity. Cities are also centers of economic growth, religion, learning, and culture.

Because each country sets its own definition of "urban", there is a bewildering array of definitions around the world. Governments of small or relatively rural countries may simply declare one or more settlements urban, regardless of size or function.[3] In many countries, the definition is based on a threshold number of inhabitants, when the population of a region exceeds a certain threshold, that region is considered urban.[4] Other governments base their definition on a combination of criteria, such as population density, political function, or predominant activity of the region.

URBAN GROWTH PATTERNS

Cities, already home to almost half the world's people, are growing rapidly in both size and number, especially in developing regions, where people flock to the cities in search of living and higher standards of living. In Asia, for example, although most people still live in rural areas, the urban population is expected to reach 2.5 billion in 2025, three times the 1990 level.[5] At present 87 Asian cities (38 of them in China, 23 in India) have more than one million people each.[6] In the past two decades the urban population has grown globally at an average rate of 4.2 per cent a year.[7]

Urbanization by itself is not the environmental issue. Instead, environmental problems arise from the urban by-products of transport, industrial activities, and the over-crowding of human habitation. The problems include pollution of air, water and accumulation of solid waste. The largest and most important cost of urban pollution is human health.

In developing world, Latin America and Caribbean constitute the most urbanized region - with more than 70 per cent of its population living in urban areas in 1995.[8] Rapid urban growth is continuing especially in small and intermediate size cities.[9] By contrast, Africa and Asia are now only about 30 to 35 per cent urban.[10] It is in these regions that the most explosive growth is under way, at roughly 4 per cent per year. This trend is projected to continue for several decades. Both Asia and Africa are expected to be about 54 per cent urban by 2025.[11]

In some respects the patterns of urban growth in developing countries are not much different from what occurred a century ago in Europe and North America. Many of the forces driving urbanization today are the same, chief among them is the shift of jobs from agriculture to industry and services and the concentration of economic opportunities in urban areas. And although cities of the developing world are growing at least twice as fast as those of developed world, yet they are not unprecedented. A number of European and U.S. cities sustained very rapid growth in the early 20th century, as fast as that now underway in the developing countries.[12]

What is unprecedented now, however, is the absolute scale of change, in terms of the number of countries undergoing rapid urbanization, the number of cities worldwide that are growing rapidly, and the sheer number of people involved.[13] Roughly 150,000 people are added to the urban population of developing countries every day.[14] Because of huge population base in developing countries, even a relatively slow rate of urban growth can mean an enormous increase in absolute numbers.

The steady increase in the level of urbanization worldwide since 1950s also reflects, to a large degree, the enormous changes in the nature and scale of economic activity worldwide. Urban growth is inextricably linked with economic growth, although it is not entirely clear which fuels which. Aggregate and *per-capita* incomes tend to be higher in more urbanized regions of the world.[15]

In addition to economic activity, major demographic forces underlie urban growth. In the earlier waves of industrialization, rapid urban growth was largely fueled by rural-to-urban migration. In the developing world today, however, the natural increase of urban population is at least as important as migration.[16] Another contributor to urban growth is the reclassification of city boundaries, which can result in dramatic changes in urban size.[17]

The importance of migration varies considerably by region, and migration flows in all directions, not just rural to urban. In some countries, rural-to-rural flows may be of larger scale than rural-to-urban.[18] Figures on rural-to-urban migration are notoriously difficult to pin down, but it is believed to account for between 40 to 60 per cent of annual urban population growth in the developing world.[19] Migration is expected to be a major factor in the coming years in regions with large rural populations, especially those where rural poverty is rampant.

Various studies suggest that the vast majority of migrants feel that relocation to the city has improved their situation, even if not as much as they might have hoped.[20] In New Delhi, a survey of poor migrants from rural areas found that their incomes were 2.5 times greater than they had been in the village, primarily because they could find about twice as many days of work in the city.[21]

Other migrants, however, are unable to find work or are forced to take ill-paying or hazardous jobs. Unable to generate enough income to meet their basic needs of food and shelter, they join the ranks of the urban poor. Hence the resultant outcome is the spontaneous, or squatter settlements which in particular tend to grow much faster than the rest of the city, with poor living conditions in terms of sanitation, drinking water, and unhealthy air to breathe.

Along with population growth have come changes in the physical dimensions of cities as they sprawl into wider regions, sometimes called "extended metropolitan regions", these include small urban centers and even rural areas outside of the urban core whose population and activities are clearly part of the functioning of the city.[22]

The industrialization process has been one of the most important transformative forces in our society. It has tremendously influenced our relations with nature and is one of the main causes of urbanization. Until about 1800, the labourer class worked in small establishments such as farms and craft workshops. The Industrial Revolution made it possible to create large production units with hundreds or even thousands of workers. This was regarded as a better use of production factors, especially of capital, in order to reach relatively low costs. The increasing size of production units created an enormous demand for labour in the near proximity of the firms, with subsequent urbanization.[23]

The world's economic system is increasingly an urban one, with overlapping networks of communication, production and trade.[24] This system with its flows of information, energy, capital, commerce, and people, provides the backbone for national development. A city's prospects or a town's- depend critically on its place within the urban system, national and international.

So does the fate of the hinterland, with its agricultural, forestry and mining, on which the urban system depends.

URBANIZATION AND ENVIRONMENT

Urban settlements being the 'engines of economic growth' and centers of economic activity make people to flock to towns and cities for better economic prospects. In this ongoing process to a larger extent a city represents the endeavour of man to free himself from the domination by nature, which in the earliest stages of human life determined his habitat to a larger degree. As centers of population and human activities, the more and more environmental problems are sprouted in cities such as :

Temperature: The temperature of a city is always warmer than that of surrounding rural areas. Temperature contrast is usually slight but difference can be as high as 10 degree Celsius in some areas. Because of this, cities are often referred to as urban heat islands. As an urban area grows, a regional heat island can develop impacting regional climate.

Temperature increase can result from numerous factors, viz. :

i) Roads, roofs and buildings conduct more heat than vegetated areas. energy builds up during the day and this stored heat is then released back to the atmosphere at night increasing temperature at the surface.

ii) The construction of roads, parking lots and buildings waterproofs the surface of a city. Channeled precipitation quickly drains into nearby storm sewers, away from the surface. Less moisture available for evaporation (which is a cooling effect) means more radiation can go into heating.

iii) There are number of heat sources within a city that can contribute to increased temperatures. Combustion of fossil fuels for industry, transportation and heating as well as human metabolism are all very concentrated in a city and supply extra heat to the atmosphere.

HIGH CONCENTRATION OF AIR POLLUTANTS

Air pollution is a major problem associated with most urban areas. It is believed that more than 1.1 billion people reside in cities with extremely poor air quality. Sources of air pollution include industrial and vehicle emissions and energy production. Often, energy use per capita is less in an urbanized area than in a rural area due to energy efficient apartments, attached housing and mass transit. The sheer number of people involved, however, still makes urban areas major contributors to air pollution. The circulation patterns associated with an urban heat island creates a dome over the city, trapping pollutants. Concentrations of pollutants such as suspended particulate matter can be thousands of times greater than rural areas.[25]

WATER RESOURCES

Urbanization can alter several aspects of the hydrosphere. Urban development causes changes in hydrology, depletion of supplies and aquatic pollution.

Hydrology: Urbanization completely alters the landscape of an area, impacting local hydrology. Roads, parking lots and buildings do not absorb precipitation as vegetation does which increases run off. In addition, the water quickly drains from streets into storm sewers. Often wetlands, which efficiently act to absorb excess water, are filled in. The development of floodplains for homes and industry, remove land where excess run off could go. With all the excess run off and lack of adequate disposal places, there is an increase in both the number and magnitude of floods. The removal of vegetation from stream banks for development leaves the water exposed to elements so that it is warmer in the summer and colder in the winter.

Consumption: Urban areas obtain their water from either surface sources or from ground water supplies. Not only does an increasing population put more demand on water resources but urbanized areas generally have a greater water demand *per-capita* than rural areas. In most urban areas the price of water is relatively low (due to government subsidies) so there is no incentive for conservation. In addition, a lot of water is lost due to old, leaky distribution systems. Those cities without easy access to surface water supplies often use ground water. This can lead to land subsidence and salinization if withdrawal rates exceed the rate of recharge.[26]

IMPAIRMENT OF WATER RESOURCES

Water pollution probably began with the foundation of the first cities 7,000 years ago along the major river systems of the Tigris-Euphrates and Indus.[27] There are many ways that urbanization contributes to the pollution of both surface and ground water. The dumping of wastes into water ways is common as they dilute and disperse pollutants. The natural processes of water flow help to break down wastes and render them harmless. But ever-increasing urban populations and their growing volume of wastes, have overtaxed the natural recycling capabilities of these waters in effective dilution and dispersal of wastes.

Urban-generated pollution comes from both localized and dispersed, or point and non-point sources. Major point sources include municipal sewage, industrial outfalls, and air emissions from power plants and heavy industries. Non-point sources include silt from earth-moving activities; storm run off from roads, home gardens, and industrial sites; infiltration from aquifers contaminated with sewage or industrial chemicals, and automobile emissions.

INDUSTRIAL POLLUTANTS

Often industry is concentrated in urban areas, particularly in the developing world. Tanneries, metal plating operations, pulp mills and refineries contribute things such as PCBs (polychlorinated biphenyls), dioxins, pesticides, grease, oil, acids and heavy metals such as cadmium and lead, sewage sludge, and a long list of synthetic organic compounds.

Urban run off is another source of industrial pollutants. As water travels over the surface it picks up pollutants from cars, fertilizers, pesticides etc. Most of the time, run off enters waterways without treatment. For some pollutants, urban run off rivals or exceeds the output from industrial sources and sewage treatment plants and is often much more difficult to track and control.[28]

SOILS AND LANDSCAPES

Approximately one per cent of the earths total land surface is urbanized. This small amount of land, however has changed drastically from its original state. Further urban expansion will destroy many more valuable habitats. Urban expansion today is often as urban sprawl, low density developments that consume vast quantities of land. The conversion of a natural landscape to an urban area is essentially an irreversible process. Some habitats that are at risk due to urbanization include, "Agricultural Lands", often agriculture and cities develop in similar areas - flat, well-drained soils close to water. Unfortunately expanding urban areas are consuming agricultural lands. Agriculture then develops in new areas that may not be as productive. In addition to destroying habitats, urbanization impacts the soil. Development of an agricultural area for agricultural purposes causes the loss of fertile top soil. The disposal of wastes is often done at sites, which can contaminate soils rendering it useless for agriculture in the future. Vehicular traffic contaminates soils with cadmium, lead, nickel, oil and grease. Paving over the surface prevents air and moisture from getting into the soil that is vital for micro-organisms and plant roots.

HEALTH AND URBANIZATION

A long range of health problems are associated with urban environmental degradation. One of thc greatest threat of the human health is the lack of adequate water and sanitation services. Inadequate access to water and sanitation facilities is the main cause for the intestinal diseases, transmitted by feces. Intestinal disorders such as diarrhea, caused by a variety of bacteria, viruses and parasites are among the most prevalent and serious health risks to children exposed to poor sanitation or contaminated water supplies. Of the 5 million children who are estimated to die annually of diarrheal diseases in the developing world, the majority come from poor urban families.[29]

Problem of waste disposal, accumulated garbage is indirectly contributing to neighbourhood environmental health problems by breeding sites for flies and other pests particularly when door-to-door waste collection is too expensive for many household or municipalities to afford and streets too narrow for vehicles collection points can easily become small garbage dumps, especially when collection is intermittent.

In an urban area sewage can be a major source of water pollution. Sewage is not only a source of nutrients, that can lead to eutrophication of water resources but it also contains many pathogens such as cholera bacterium, hepatitis viruses, salmonellae, and shigellas which pose a significant risk to health.[30]

Recent studies give strong evidence of the relationship between air pollution and premature death.[31] Since the late 1970s, epidemiological data from cities in the United States have consistently suggested that air pollution kills primarily through respiratory or cardiovascular disease about 30,000 to 60,000 people per year, accounting directly for 2 to 3 per cent of all deaths.[32]

In those cities with high air pollution levels and a combination of geography and weather that prevents pollutants from dispersing, ambient air pollution can pose significant health risks to rich and poor alike.

Suspended particulate matter is nearly ubiquitous urban pollutant, a complex mixture of small and large particles of varying origin and chemical composition. Larger particles ranging from about 2.5 microns to 100 microns in diameter, usually comprise smoke and dust from industrial processes, agriculture, construction, and road traffic, as well as plant pollen and other natural sources. Smaller particles those less than 2.5 microns in diameter generally come from combustion of fossil fuels. These particles include soot from vehicle exhaust, which is often coated with various chemical contaminants or metals, and fine sulphate and nitrate aerosols that form when Sulphur dioxide (SO_2) and Nitrogen oxides condense in the atmosphere. The largest source of fine particles is coal-fired power plants, but auto and diesel exhaust are also prime contributors, especially along busy transportation corridors. The health effects of particulates are strongly linked to particle size. Small particles, such as those from fossil fuel combustion, are likely to be most dangerous, because, they can be inhaled deeply into the lungs, settling in areas where the body's natural clearance mechanisms cannot remove them. The constituents in small particulates also tend to be more chemically active and may be acidic as well and therefore more damaging.[33]

Numerous studies associate particulate pollution with acute changes in lung function and respiratory illness.[34] Resulting in increased hospital admissions for respiratory disease and heart disease, school and job absences from respiratory infections, or aggravation of chronic conditions such as asthma and bronchitis.[35]

Worldwide, an estimated 1.1 billion urban residents are exposed to particulate or Sulphur dioxide levels in excess of the guidelines set by the World Health Organization (WHO).[36]

The World Health Organization (WHO) estimated that short-term pollution exposure accounted for 7 to 10 per cent of all lower respiratory illnesses in children, with the number rising to 21 per cent in the most polluted cities. Furthermore, 0.6 to 1.6 per cent of deaths were attributable to short-term pollution events, climbing to 3.4 per cent in the cities with the dirtiest air.[37]

In the cities where residential or industrial coal use is still prevalent and diesel traffic is heavy SO_2 is largely emitted into atmosphere. Epidemiological studies indicate that SO_2 exposure can lead to the kind of acute health effects typical of particulate pollution. Exposure is linked to an increase in hospitalizations and deaths from respiratory and cardiovascular causes, especially among asthmatics and those with pre-existing respiratory diseases.[38] The severity of these effects increases with rising SO_2 levels, and exercise enhances the severity by increasing the volume of SO_2 inhaled and allowing SO_2 to penetrate deeper into the respiratory tract.[39] Asthmatics may experience wheezing and other symptoms at much lower SO_2 levels than those without asthma. When ozone pollution is also present, asthmatics become problematic. Ozone at the ground level is formed when nitrogen oxides from fuel combustion react with so-called Volatile Organic Compounds (VOCs) such as unburned gasoline or paint solvents in the atmosphere.

In countries where auto and industrial emissions have increased, ozone pollution has become widespread. Many cities in the developing countries also suffer from high ozone levels, although few monitoring data exists.[40]

Breathing ozone concentrations of 0.012 ppm levels typical in many cities can irritate the respiratory tract and impair lung function, causing coughing, shortness of breath, and chest pain. Exercise increases these effects, and heavy exercise can bring on symptoms even at low ozone levels (0.08 ppm). Evidence also suggests ozone exposure lowers body's defenses; increasing susceptibility to respiratory infections.[41] Lead is one of the hazardous elements which is ubiquitous in the urban environment. Emissions from vehicles burning leaded gasoline, industrial emissions, particularly form smelters and battery recycling plants, are significant sources. Humans are exposed to lead via inhalation of contaminated air, ingestion of contaminated water and foods. Lead's principle threat other than acute lead poisoning is neurological damage in children. A 1988 study in Mexico City, where ambient lead levels are high because of the use of leaded gasoline, found that more than one quarter of new borns had blood lead levels high enough to impair neurological and motor-physical development.[42]

Occupational hazards can be significant addition to the health burdens that urban life imposes. These can include contact with a wide range of toxic substances, unsafe machinery, unhealthful noise levels, inadequate lighting or ventilation, and extremes of heat or cold. These hazards are often made worse by a lack of protective clothing or equipment.[43]

In many developing countries, the problem of occupational hazards is compounded by the lack of any sick pay or compensation for workplace injuries, as well as a lack of adequate occupational health care.[44] In developing nations of Asia and Africa, less than 25 percent of the workforce is thought to have access to any kind of occupational health service.[45]

The most common occupational disease include respiratory diseases caused by particulates such as asbestos; silicon and cotton; metal poisoning from lead; pesticide poisoning; hearing loss from excessive noise and skin diseases due to chemical exposures.[46]

In some instances, disease rates among exposed workers can be very high. In asbestos factories in Bombay, one third of the workers suffered from asbestos-related disease, according to a 1983 report.[47]

Health hazards in the work place may be exacerbated by malnutrition or the burden of chronic diseases that workers already suffer from, both of which may lower resistance to toxic contaminants or infectious diseases encountered at work.

Hazards may also be intensified by climatic conditions, such as hot and humid weather, which make it more difficult to convince workers to use protective clothing such as respirators or aprons. Long working hours frequently demanded by employers or opted by the workers themselves for financial reasons, can play a part in increasing exposures to chemical toxins or increasing accident rates due to fatigue.[48]

An unpolluted, healthy environment is the Fundamental Right of everyone. In urban environment, health, in its broadest sense of physical, mental and spiritual well-being is to a great extent dependent on the access of the citizen to environmental assets conducive to well-being.

URBAN SCENARIO IN INDIA

It was not till the middle of the third millennium B.C. that true urban life found its full expression in India and it began first in the valley of the Indus - now in Pakistan with its mature phase at the principal site of Mohenjo-daro dated to 2500 B.C.[49,50]

The urban development, designated by the archaeologists as the 'Harappa Culture', found its full expression in the two metropolitan cities of Mohenjo-daro and Harappa. The two cities, nearly four hundred miles apart, acted as the twin capitals of the Indus Empire.[51] Being more than three miles in the circuit, both have remarkable uniformity in their physical setting, internal layout, basic architecture, sanitary arrangements, street planning, etc.[52] Strict enforcement of building regulation is observed in all the earlier phases of construction when buildings were never allowed to encroach upon the public thoroughfares.[53] In town planning the first thing that strikes the eye is the street planning. A principle of coordinated measurement used to be stubbornly followed in the construction of the streets so that the largest about 45 ft wide was twice the width of the smaller, and three or four times that of the side lanes. The alignment of the streets from east to west and from north to south at Mohenjo-daro is thought to have been purposely made for keeping the urban area properly ventilated under the prevailing north-south winds.[54] The cities are furnished with an elaborate underground drainage system. House drains are connected with the street drains by earthenware pipes and latter used to be cleared through manholes. The city's sewage finally found its way into soak-pits which ultimately emptied into the river. All these signify the existence of a strict municipal vigilance.[55] What is curious to note is that such a high grade civilization utterly failed to transmit the rich ideas concerning planning, architecture, civic amenity services or even sculpture to their successors. The only field reflecting the continuity of this culture to a little degree is religion. The reasons are perhaps, too obvious to be ignored. Since the fall of the Indus cities the overall situation of the country was not favorable for a long time for the emergence of urban culture. Apart from being the 'city-destroyers' - a term happily and frequently used by the Aryans for themselves in the text of the Rigveda, they were no lovers of urban life of which they had no practical experience when they came to India.[56]

It is to be noted that, the word 'nagra' (city) does not occur in the early hymns of Rigveda nor there is any mention of individual cities as is found in latter texts.[57] The colonization, or better to call it the land grab policy of the Aryans, vastly extending their domain gradually made village federations which, in the long run, became quite inefficient in keeping effective control over their possessions. This supplemented further by community feuds, resulted in the rise of kingdoms, defining the territorial limits of different groups or dynasties, such consolidation of the Aryan tribal system into large or small kingdoms made the most important contribution to the urban history of India as it was only then that some of the village settlements, serving the purpose of royal capitals of kingdoms, ultimately developed into towns and cities. In many ways this may be called the real beginning of urbanization in country for two reasons : first, from this period onwards there had been no break in the history of urban development, though, at times, the progress had been extremely tardy and faltering; second, quite a number of towns and cities born at this time, inspite of many vicissitudes, have maintained their existence down to this day which, as it will be found time and again, is also equally true about many of the later ones born at different periods of the succeeding centuries.

During the Maurya and Gupta periods urban environment excelled with public buildings, fine gardens, imposing temples and provisions of water and sanitation.[58] The Mughal period likewise saw a golden age of monumental architecture of palaces, forts and mosques, beautiful gardens and others with an overtone of grandeur and pomp.[59] The British period ushered in the present urban environment with trading and administrative functions which improved and deteriorated simultaneously in the industrial era.[60]

With the development of roads, villagers have become more accustomed to visiting nearby centers for shopping, trade, education and medical care. The considerable floating population of big cities also contributes to the increasingly urban character of the nearby villages. Since 1947 the nation has embarked on a programme of rapid industrialization, and, by and large, industries continue to locate in the cities. Workers from villages are drawn in, not all of them from nearby areas. Cities also attract large number of domestic and other servants, and people to work in shops, restaurants, and other small businesses.

So in the wake of rapid urban population growth, particularly following the implementation of governmental comprehensive Industrial Policy and the first of Five Year Plans in 1951 the percentage of the population living in urban areas rose from 17.3 in 1951 to 19.9 in 1971, to 23.3 in 1981 to 30 per cent in 1995 (see Table A).

LEVEL OF URBANIZATION

The overall effect of this rapid growth of urban population took the following manifestations.

(a) Slums

Growth has overtaken the cities' capacity to plan, with the result that ugly and unhygienic slums have proliferated. The slums frequently exist cheek by jowl with fancy apartments and the bungalows of the rich. Some of the new housing, intended for low or even middle class people is dreary beyond description. Rows of apartment buildings, unrelieved by trees or shrubs, mar the landscape in bigger cities. Above all as many as 25% to 30% of the urban population live in slums and squatter settlements. This problem is particularly more acute in Calcutta, Bombay,

Table (A). Key Statistics of Urbanization in India, 1901-91

Census Year	No. of towns	Urban Population (millions)	Urbanization level (%)	Percentage urban population in towns 20,000 or more persons	Intercensal annual growth rate (%) Urban population	Intercensal annual growth rate (%) Rural population	Difference between urban and rural growth rates
1901	1,916	25.9	10.8	52.9	-	-	-
1911	1,908	25.9	10.3	55.4	0.0	0.6	-0.6
1921	2,048	28.1	11.2	56.1	0.8	-0.1	0.9
1931	2,220	33.5	12.0	59.7	1.7	1.0	0.7
1941	2,422	44.2	13.8	66.0	28.0	1.1	1.7
1951	3,060	62.4	17.3	70.4	3.5	0.8	2.6
1961	2,700	78.9	18.0	79.6	2.3	1.9	0.4
1971	3.126	109.1	19.9	84.1	3.2	2.0	1.2
1981	4,029	159.5	23.3	86.4	3.8	1.8	2.0
1991	4,688	217.6	25.7	89.4	3.1	1.8	1.3

Notes : Number of towns shown above is taken from Planning Commission, Eighth Five Year Plan, Vol. 2, p. 345.

Sources : Census of India 1991, Series 1, Paper 2 of 1991, Provisional Population Totals: Rural Urban Distribution. Also Census of India 1971, Series 1 - India, Part II - A(i) General Population Tables; Census of India, 1981, Series-1, India, Part B(i), Primary Census Abstract : General Population: Census of India, 1981, Series-1, Paper-1 of 1982, Final Population Totals.

Delhi and Madras.[61] These settlements are often devoid of adequate water supply, sewage and drainage facilities and waste disposal services. Second, these people live in crowded and cramped conditions under which communicable diseases can flourish, particularly when malnutrition lowers resistance. Marshall B. Clinard states that : "in the slums of India, however, the drains are generally open, the water is usually stagnant because of poor gradients and choked drains present sickening sights and offensive odours. Refuse is everywhere, and the few available containers are seldom properly used. More often trash, garbage and refuse are shored into the drains or left on the streets... the drains, and the children usually use them as latrines... their excreta, because of the very high incidence of disease among them, are the chief means of spreading such diseases as dysentery and cholera among the populace."[62]

(b) Street Children

Another pathetic outcome of the urbanization is street children. According to UNICEF Report, "street children are a phenomenon of modern times when urban centres in developing countries are faced with the process of rapid urbanization."[63] Worth to mention here is that it is chronic poverty, unemployment, overcrowded homes, broken families, drug abuse, alcoholism... some of the factors associated with urbanization which make a stressful situation for a child at home and later on drifting him into the streets. Most of these children, for survival, choose occupations such as shining shoes, washing cars, and rag picking (i.e., sorting and collecting rags, plastics, paper, etc. from refuse thrown on the pavements and dump sites and selling it to the middle men or recycling shops) constitutes major occupational categories for street children, which is surely the most de-humanising occupation where the nature of work and the work environment are most unhygienic, dangerous, and destructive of self growth.

(c) Epidemics

In September 1994, nearly 30 years after last urban

outbreak of plague in India, plague struck Surat, a city in the western part of India.[64] The Surat outbreak, which killed 56 people nationwide, did not have the devastating impact originally feared, but it did generate considerable anxiety worldwide while also exacting a heavy economic toll in India.[65] It also served as a chilling reminder of how rapid urbanization and deterioration of the urban environment can bring people into contact with forgotten disease vectors.

Plague has long been a scourge of cities. The disease, caused by the bacterium Yersinia pests, is best known for its role in the Black Death that swept across Europe and Asia in middle ages, killing roughly one fourth of the population of Western Europe - an estimated 20 million people. Yet, its roots may be more ancient still: as early as 1190 BC, Homer referred to a plague like disease that was associated with the movement of rats into populated areas.[66]

The last major epidemic occurred early in the 20th century in India, resulting in the death of more than 10 million people.[67] There are two types of plague - Bubonic plague and Pneumonic plague. Bubonic plague is transmitted to people through the bite of an infected flea. In urban areas, rats are primary source of plague-infected fleas. The outbreak of plague that occurred in Surat was pneumonic plague - a highly contagious form of disease that kills 100 per cent of its victims if left untreated. Pneumonic plague is caused by same disease organism that causes bubonic plague, but it infects the lungs rather than lymph system. Since the disease invades the lungs it can be transmitted to others in close physical contact through exhaled sputum droplets. Crowding and poor sanitation can provide ideal conditions for the spread of this type of plague.[68]

A year before the plague incident at Surat, an earthquake measuring 6.4 on the Richter scale hit the adjacent State of Maharashtra, killing at least 10,000 people and causing extensive damage.[69] Researchers believe that the disturbances and resettlement associated with the earthquake helped bring the wild rodent population inhabiting the forested area near Surat into contact with the domestic rat population, introducing the disease into the local rat population in the process. Surat's sanitation problem then helped the rat population grow dramatically. Surat, a city of 2.2 million, generates close to 1,250 metric tons of garbage each day, 250 metric tons of which remain uncollected. To make matters worse, flood waters inundated the city during the 1994 monsoon, particularly in low lying slum areas near the river. Surat residents complain that nothing was done to remove the huge piles of rubbish that remained after the flood waters receded, offering an ideal habitat for rats.

The re-emergence of plague is a striking reminder that infectious diseases have not been defeated. Malaria has consolidated its strength as a major killer, although it had almost disappeared a few decades ago. Cholera and tuberculosis are donning new faces with drug resistant strains. By comparison, the health toll of the Surat plague was relatively minor. It killed 56 people whereas the malaria epidemic in Rajasthan in 1994 killed nearly 300 people.[70]

(d) Housing Scenario

The rapid pace of urbanization, coupled with rapid population growth and the inadequacy of available infrastructure is causing many serious consequences on the health and quality of life of its citizens. The quality of life depends on the quality of civic amenities available to the citizens. This is true of all the citizens irrespective of their socio-economic status or area of residence. There are certain basic amenities like, housing, drinking water, sanitation, recreation, streets which can be considered as basic needs of the people or essential components which exert an impact on the health status of the population. This fact had also been recognised by the United Nations which, in its "Report on International Definition and Measurement of Standards and Levels of Living", 1954 (Sales No. 54.iv.5), had identified, *inter alia*, "Health including demographic conditions" and

"Housing including housing facilities" as essential components of level of living.

Housing not only means shelter but to fulfill social, educational and economic functions.[71] It provides a physical base for family activities and a personal territory for which the family can gradually extend its involvement in urban affairs, particularly in the case of recent in-migration to the city.[72] Studies on the impact of housing conditions on health have documented strong negative associations of inadequate quantity and quality of water supply, sanitation facilities, space, ventilation etc., in the dwelling unit with the health of its inhabitants.[73]

The World Health Organization in one of its publication summarizes the health implications of housing in the following statements:

"Housing is intimately related to health. The structure, location, facilities, environment and uses of human shelter having a strong impact on the state of physical, mental and social well being. Poor housing conditions and uses may provide weak defenses against death, disease and injury or even increase vulnerability to them. Adequate and appropriate housing conditions, on the other hand, not only protect people against health hazards but also help to promote robust physical health, economic productivity, psychological well-being and social vigour."[74]

The National Commission on Urbanization, in its report submitted to the Government of India, in August 1988, has observed: "the most visible and dehumanising manifestations of India's urbanization is the largest number of squatters and shanty dwellers so ubiquitous in all our major cities. The cause of this distressing situation is deep-rooted in wide-ranging factors, from building regulations to economic growth policies."[75]

In India the existing housing situation leaves much to be desired both in terms of quality and quantity. The country has been facing acute shortage of housing, particularly in large cities, for last several decades. The estimated shortage of houses at the beginning of the seventh plan was about 25.0 million units, out of which about 6.0 million were required for urban areas.[76] By 1990, the shortage was expected to grow to 9.7 million units in urban areas. In Delhi alone, which has a population increase from 2.0 to 9.0 million between 1957 and 1990, there is an addition of 60,000 people each year who need to be provided with new housing.[77] According to UNI report almost 70 per cent of Delhi's population live in sub-standard conditions.[78]

The ever-widening gap between the demand and supply of housing in urban areas has severely affected the living conditions of city dwellers. Extreme overcrowding dilapidated structures, absence of basic minimum amenities in the dwellings and the lack of basic services in residential localities are common features of living conditions in all large cities in India.[79]

The United Nations Commission on Human Settlements (UNCHS), at the Hague in November 1990, identifies four sustainable development criteria for judging a settlement:

i) The quality of life it offers to its inhabitants;

ii) The scale of non-renewable resources use (including the extent to which secondary sources are drawn form settlement by-products for re-use);

iii) The scale and nature of renewable resource use and the implications for sustaining production levels of renewable resources;

iv) The scale and nature of non-reusable wastes generated by production and consumption activities and the means by which these are disposed off, including the extent to which wastes impact on human health, natural systems and amenity.

On this basis, the Declaration observed that the role of human management in promoting sustainable development includes :

i) Devising settlement-system and settlement plans which lead to resource-efficient and affording transport patterns;

ii) Developing programmes for economizing the use of non-renewable energy sources and for adapting settlements to the use of renewable energy systems;

iii) Providing water supply, sanitation, waste processing and recycling systems which meet basic needs in a resource conserving manner;

iv) Promoting the use of indigenous building materials and appropriate construction technologies, *inter alia*, by revising building and planning codes and supporting small-scale production process.

On this basic premise, the declaration identifies sector level actions for water supply, sanitation, solid waste management initiatives for making development meet the sustainability criteria.

The UNCHS in connection with its sustainable cities programme define a sustainable city as '...... a city where achievements in social, economic and physical development are made to last' and city 'which .... has a lasting supply of natural resources on which its development depends and a lasting security from environmental hazards which may threaten development achievements' (UNCHS, 1991).

URBAN PLANNING

At the micro level, the solution to urban problems is, to a large extent, dependent upon the disposition and approach of urban planning. In 1962 Delhi was given a twenty year Master Plan (MP) (1961-81) and Calcutta got the Basic Development Plan (BDP 1966-86) in 1965.[80] At the conceptual plane, the Master Plan approach, developed in Europe in the thirties and later abandoned due to its limitations, was transplanted into Indian cities without considering its relevance. First, it evolved during the Depression of thirties and hence it has an inbuilt value premise of going slow and steady. Indian cities, on the contrary, have been experiencing an explosive demographic growth which the static disposition of the MP approach is unable to cope with. Second, the MP is concerned with land use, city form and zoning regulation which have a negative policy stance. Instead of promoting the development of various organs of the city system, the MP tries to restrain and control it and this process is heavy on both time and resources. Third, MP is essentially a remote long range, rigid plan. It therefore suffers from the deficiency of attempting to foresee the purposes, needs and situation of an urban settlement — a complicated organism — some twenty years ahead. Thus it cannot comprehend the emergence of any unexpected event or new situation which could alter its long range vision. Its long term approach and rigidity does not enable it to provide solutions to the problems within the dynamic situation in which the towns and cities have to live. Fourth, the MP, being pre-occupied with control system, is hardly concerned with the problems of shelter and urban poverty so rampant in third world cities. The deprived, the downtrodden, the low income strata and the urban informal sector which provides them with source of livelihood, do not find any place in the priorities of the planners. The deprived, therefore, create their own autonomous settlements causing 'chaotic' and 'haphazard' growth which the plans intend to solve. To give an illustration from Delhi, "out of about 63,000 acres of land to be acquired in order to implement the Master Plan for Delhi (1961-81), about 3,000 acres of land could not be acquired because of their unauthorised occupation. The slow pace of land development and prohibitive land prices that the urban poor and low income groups cannot afford, led to the growth of about 1000 unauthorised squatter settlements housing about 1.5 million people.[81]"

CONCLUSION

Many problems of urban development in India can be tackled at least partially by convincing the beneficiaries or users of services about the simple fact of life that there can be no 'free lunch' for any society. The delivery of services of high quality cannot be ensured without recovering at least the variable costs (including maintenance) and in the long run without paying also for the fixed or developmental costs which would contribute towards an expansion of the infrastructure.

The urban local bodies also need to strengthen their capacity for enforcing the basic regulations in regard to land encroachment; traffic laws; pollution of water, air and land; as well as waste disposal. On one hand, the cities are growing at a rapid pace, and on the other hand, the capacity of the roads is limited with the number of vehicles ever increasing, resulting in slowing down of vehicular speeds, unbearable air pollution and increase in the number of road accidents. The commuter today is a harassed person and is tired when he reaches the work place. The quality of life has immensely suffered. It is high time that the issue of providing adequate transport system is viewed in proper perspective without any further delay.

Enumerating the advantages of Mass Rapid Transit System (MRTS) over other modes of public transports, it is imperative that Rail-based transport system may be given higher degree of importance as the system provides higher carrying capacity, faster, smoother and safer travel, occupy less space, are non-polluting and energy efficient.

The plague epidemic that began in Surat in 1994 had created a serious scare in India about the consequence of unregulated urban growth.[82] These problems cannot be ignored for long in view of the imminent large additions to the urban population. In a long run perspective, a simultaneous effort at a balanced rural and urban development, which narrows (and eventually eliminates) the differentials in the basic amenities available to the people of different areas, is imperative.

For preparing the management plans for the urban areas, the cause of the pollution problems is to be identified and solutions provided for short-term mitigation measures and long-term prevention measures. This may be done through environmental management plans. The objective of preparing such plans are :

i) To map the characteristics and environmental profile of an urban area and to identify the environmental pollution hot spots;

ii) To prepare an environmental management plan that includes rehabilitation and mitigation measures; and

iii) To recommend guidelines for environmentally compatible land use planning.

The study area for preparation of an environmental management plan should include the main city and its immediate vicinity upto where the activities of the city are spread. Such an area is generally termed as 'urban area'. The broad approach for preparation of the environmental management plan involves the following steps :

i) Mapping of the characteristics and environmental profile of the urban area;

ii) Identification of the pollution 'hot spots';

iii) Recommendation of pollution mitigation measures and abatement infrastructure; and

iv) Recommending land use controls compatible to the pollution sources.

The uses to be considered while preparing management plans are:

i) Trade and industry locations;

ii) Transport facilities;

iii) Refuse/hazardous waste, wastewater installations;

iv) Quarrying/mining;

v) Agriculture;

vi) Recreation and tourism;

vii) Power generation;

viii) Housing construction;

ix) Forestry

PRIORITY ACTION

To ensure balanced growth and development of urban areas free from environmental degradation it is necessary to frame effective and rational development policies, viz.

i) Regional plan/development policies should be framed;

ii) Master plan preparation should be in conformity with the regional plan/developmental policies;

iii) Actions should be initiated for achieving integrated urban development __ various departments and expert organisations should be involved in preparing sectoral plans - and planning should aim at developmental targets of various departments (participatory approach);

iv) For the urban areas (especially those with environmental problems) environmental management plans should be prepared, action plans drawn and responsible organisations and budgetary requirements identified for implementation. Actions also need regular monitoring of environmental factors/considerations should be incorporated into planning and development process;

v) Space requirements have to be identified for the infrastructure facilities of sewage-network, treatment, disposal, solid waste-collection, treatment/disposal etc. and incorporated into urban planning innovative technologies that are cost-effective;

vi) Environmental Cells in the departments will go a long way in improving the present situation;

vii) It is equally incumbent that the poor and underprivileged classes of society get a fair deal in the matter of housing and enjoyment of common physical environment;

viii) To curb undue rise in land values and prevent land speculation; and

ix) Above all mass awareness programmes should be launched for mobilising people towards creating a better environment worthy decent living.

These are the minimum requirements to ensure the preservation of necessary components of sustainable urban development. A healthy environment is the Fundamental Right of everyone. In urban environment, health, in its broadest sense of physical, mental and spiritual well-being, is to a great extent dependent on the access of the citizen to environment and its conducive to well-being.

REFERENCES

1. H.D. Kopardekar, *Social Aspects of Urban Development, A Case Study of the pattern of Urban Development in the Developing Countries*, Bombay Popular Prakashan, 1986, p. 16.
2. Philip M. Hanser, Leo F. Schnore, *The Study of Urbanization*, John Wiley and Sons, Inc., New York, 1965, p. 521.
3. Jorge E. Hardoy and David Satterthwaite, "Urban Change in the Third World : Are recent Trends a Useful Pointer to the Urban Future?" *Habitat International*, Vol. 10, No. 3 (1986), p. 34.
4. *Ibid.*
5. *1999 World Development Indicators*, The World Bank, p. 116.
6. *Ibid.*
7. *Ibid.*
8. United Nations Population Division, World Urbanization Prospects : The 1994 Revision (U.N. New York, 1995), pp. 91, 107.
9. Jorge Gavidia, "Housing and Land in Large Cities of Latin America", in Enhancing the Management of Metropolitan Living Environments in Latin America (United Nations

Centre for Human Development, Nagoya, Japan 1994), p. 19.

10. *Supra note* 8, pp. 87, 89, 103, 105.
11. *Ibid.*
12. United Nations Centre for Human Settlements (Habitat), *An Urbanizing World : Global Report on Human Settlements 1996* (Oxford University Press, Oxford, United Kingdom).p. 127.
13. *Ibid.*, pp. 1-28.
14. United Nations (U.N.) Population Division, *Op.cit.*, p. 27.
15. The World Bank, *Urban Policy and Economic Development : An Agenda for the 1990s* (The World Bank, Washington, D.C., 1991), p. 18.
16. United Nations Centre for Human Settlements (Habitat), *Op.cit.*, p. 124.
17. Terence G. McGee and C.J. Griffiths, "Global Urbanization : Towards the Twenty First Century", in Population Distribution and Migration, draft proceedings of the United Nations Expert Meeting on Population Distribution and Migration, Santa Cruz, Bolivia, January 18, 1993, p. 22.
18. *Supra note 12*, pp. 1-24.
19. Terence G. McGee and C.J. Griffiths, *Op.cit.*, p. 60.
20. Josef Gugler, "Overurbanizaiton Reconsidered", *The Urbanization of the Third World*, Oxford University Press, Oxford, United Kingdom, 1988, p. 83.
21. Mike Parnwell, *Population Movements and the Third World,* Routledge, London, 1993, p. 87.
22. *Supra note* 12, pp. 1-18.
23. Hans G.T. Van Raay, Aricl E. Lugo, *Man and Environment Ltd., Natural Imbalances and Social Justice*, Rotlerdam University Press, 1974, p. 159.
24. *Our Common Future*, The World Commission on

Environment and Development, Oxford University Press, Delhi, 1987, p. 235.

25. http://royal.okanagan.bc.ca/mpidwirn/urbanization/urbanization.html
26. *Ibid.*
27. Michael Meybeck, Deborah Chapman, and Richard Helmer, eds., Global Freshwater Quality : A First Assessment (United Nations Environment Programme and World Health Organization, Geneva, 1989), p. 42.
28. Robert Adler, "Reauthorizing the Clean Water Act : Looking to Tangible Values", *Water Resources Bulletin*, Oklahoma, Vol. 30, No. 5 (1994), p. 802.
29. World Health Organization (WHO), Commission on Health and Environment, Report of the Panel on Urbanization (WHO, Geneva, 1992), p. 67.
30. United Nations Economic and Social Commission for Asia and Pacific, State of the Environment in Asia and Pacific, 1990 (U.N., Bangkok, Thailand, 1992), p. 60.
31. C. Arden Pope III et al., "Particulate Air Pollution as a Predictor of Mortality in a Prospective Study of U.S. Adults", *American Journal of Respiratory and Critical Care Medicine*, New York, Vol. 151, No. 3 (March 1995), p. 669, p. 674.
32. Philip J. Hilts, "Studies Say Soot Kills up to 60,000 in U.S. Each Year", *New York Times* (July 19, 1993), p. A1.
33. World Health Organization (WHO), Update and Revision of the Air Quality Guideline for Europe, WHO Regional Office for Europe, Report No. EUR/ICP/EHAZ 94-05/PB01 (WHO, Copenhagen, 1994), p. 15.
34. Douglas Dockery, et al., "Health Effects of Acid Aerosols on North American Children: Respiratory Symptoms", *Environmental Health Perspectives*, North Carolina USA, Vol. 104, No. 5, 1996, p. 503.

35. Dcborah Shprcntz, Brcathtaking: Prcmaturc Mortality Duc to Particulate Air Pollution in 239 American Cities (Natural Resources Defense Council, New York, 1996), pp. 14-15.

36. Dietrich Schwela, "Public Health Implication of Urban Air Pollution in Developing Countries: paper presented at the 10th World Clean Air Congress, Erjos, Finland, May 28 - June 2, 1995, p. 1.

37. R. Bertollini et al., *Environment and Health 1: Overview and Main European Issues*, WHO Regional Publications, European Series, No. 68 (World Health Organization, Copenhagen, 1996), pp. 34-38.

38. A. Peters et al., "Acute Effects of Exposure to High Levels of Air Pollution in Eastern Europe", *American Journal of Epidemiology*, Maryland, Vol. 144, No. 6, 1996, pp. 570, 578-90.

39. M. Vigotti *et al.*, "Short Term Effects of Urban Air Pollution on Respiratory Health in Milan, Italy 1980-1989", *Journal of Epidemiology and Community Health*, The Netherlands, Vol. 50 (Supplement 1) (April 1996), p. 87.

40. World Health Organization and the United Nations Environment Programme, *Urban Air Pollution in Mega cities of the World* Blackwell Publishers, Oxford, UK, 1992, pp. 10-11.

41. Haluk Ozkaynak et al., Ambient Ozone Exposure and Emergency Hospital Admissions and Emergency Room Visits for Respiratory Problems in 13 U.S. Cities (American Lung Association, Washington D.C., 1996), pp. 2-7.

42. David Satterthwaite, "The Impact on Health of Urban Environment", *Environment and Urbanization*, London, Vol. 5, No. 2, (October 1993), p. 93.

43. Choon-Nam Ong, Jesry Jeyaratnam, and David Koh, "Factors Influencing the Assessment and Control of

Occupational Hazards in Developing Countries", *Environmental Research*, Vol. 60, No. 1 (Jan. 1, 1993), pp. 112, 123.

44. Jorge Hardoy, Diana Mitlin, and David Satterthwaite, *Environmental Problems in Third World Cities,* Earthscan, London, 1992, p. 49.
45. Choon-Nan Ong, *Op.cit.*, p. 114.
46. Eric Chivian et al., eds. *Human Health and the Environment*, MIT Press, Cambridge, Massachusetts, 1993, pp. 74, 77.
47. Jorge Hardoy, Diana Mitlin, *Op.cit.*, pp. 49, 50.
48. Choon-Nam Ong, *Op.cit.*, pp. 116, 117.
49. Rao, S.R., *Lothal and Indus Civilization,* Asia Publishing House, London, 1972, p. 207.
50. Wheeler, Mortimer, *Civilization of the Indus valley and Beyond*, Thames and Hudson, London, 1966, p. 72.
51. Bridget and Allchin, *The Birth of Indian Civilization, India and Pakistan before 500 B.C.*, Penguin Books, 1968, p. 129.
52. Piggot, Staurt, *Prehistoric India to 1000 B.C.*, Penguin Press, 1961, p. 158.
53. Prof. B. Bhattacharya, *Urban Development in India (Since Prehistoric times)*, Shree Publishing House, Delhi, 1979, p. 30.
54. Mackey, Ernest, *Early Indus Civilization* (Revised and Enlarged by Dorothy Mackay), Ideological Book Corporation, Delhi, 1976, p. 19.
55. Wheeler, Mortimer, *Op.cit.*, p. 24.
56. Urban Development in India, *Op.cit.*, p. 66.
57. Majumdar, R.C., Ray Chaudhuri, H.C. Datta, K., *An Advanced History of India*, Third Edition, Macmillan, 1970, pp. 32-33.

58. M.M. Jana, *Environmental Degradation and Development Strategies in India*, Ashish Publishing House, New Delhi, 1991, p. 220.
59. *Ibid.*
60. *Ibid.*
61. Nagpaul Hans, "The Slum and Squatter Settlements in Metropolitan India; Review of Some Strategies for Better Urban Environment", *Indian Journal of Social Research*; Meerut, Vol. 23, No. 1, April 1982, pp. 1-28.
62. As cited by Basu Ghosh in *Health Implications of Public Policy*, Indian Institute of Management, Bangalore, Feb. 1991, p. 291.
63. Street Children of Bangalore, A Study conducted for Ministry of Social Welfare Govt. of India and UNICEF, By Ms. N. Reddy, Published by National Labour Institute, Noida, p. 4.
64. John W. Anderson, "Plague Deaths Recede in Stricken Indian City", *Washington Post*, September 27, 1994, p. A10.
65. Centers for Disease Control and Prevention, "Update: Human Plague - India, 1994", *Morbidity and Mortality Weekly Report*, Vol. 43, No. 41, October 21, 1994.
66. Joshua Lederberg et al. eds., *Institute of Medicine, Emerging Infections : Microbial Threats to Health in the United States*, National Academy Press, Washington, D.C., 1992, pp. 16-17.
67. *Ibid.*, p. 16.
68. Tom Post et al., "The Plague of Panic", *Newsweek*, New York, October 10, 1994, pp. 40-41.
69. V.K. Saxena et al., "Earthquake in Maharashtra : Impact Assessment on Communicable Diseases Potential", *Journal of Basic and Applied Medicine*, Vol. 2, No. 1, 1993, p. 77.

70. World Health Organization, "India Malaria", *Weekly Epidemiological Record*, Vol. 69, No. 43, October 28, 1994, p. 321.

71. John D. Herbert, *Urban Development in the Third World, Policy Guidelines*, Praeger Publishers, New York, 1979, p. 73.

72. *Ibid.*

73. WHO Housing - The implications for health, Report of a WHO Consultation, WHO, Geneva, 1987.

74. WHO, Health Principles of Housing, WHO, Geneva, 1989.

75. National Commission on Urbanization, Report of the National Commission on Urbanization, Vol. II, Govt. of India, New Delhi, Aug. 1988.

76. As cited by Ram Ahuja in *Social Problems in India*, Rawat Publications, Jaipur, 1992, p. 258.

77. *Ibid.*

78. *The Hindustan Times*, 9th May, 1988.

79. Basu Ghosh, *Op.cit.*, p. 259.

80. As cited by K.S. Shukla in *The Other Side of Development, Social Psychological Implications*, Sage Publications, New Delhi, 1987, p. 170.

81. Gangadhar Jha, "Land Nationalisation in Delhi : A Policy Analysis", *Nagarlok*, New Delhi, Vol. 15, No. 2, April-June 1983b, pp. 9-26.

82. Pravin Visaria, *Urbanization in Large Developing Countries*, Claredon Press, Oxford, 1997, p. 287.

6
Conclusion

Human right is a concept that has been constantly evolving throughout human history. It has been intricately tied to the life of individuals and social and economic laws, customs and religions throughout the ages. It was in ancient Greece where the concept of human rights began to take a greater meaning than the prevention of arbitrary prosecution. Human rights became synonymous with Racial and Natural Rights, rights that spring from Natural Law. The Doctrine of Natural Rights passed into the realm of practical reality when an absolute monarch of England himself (King John) was made to acknowledge that there are certain rights of the subject which could not be eroded even by a Sovereign in whom all powers were legally vested.

The Doctrine of Natural Rights received further impetus at the hands of the great protagonist of the theory of social contract, particularly Locke and Rousseau, who sought to trace the genesis of political society and government in an agreement into which individuals entered to form a collective society to ensure their personal and general interest and the objects, but at the same time without interfering with their 'Natural Rights' which already belonged to them as human beings.

The Declaration of Independence in United States, adopted on July 4, 1776, expresses the "Natural Rights" idea in these memorable words: "We hold these truths to be self-evident, that all Men are created equal, that they are endowed by their Creator with certain Inalienable Rights, that among these are Life, Liberty, and the Pursuit of Happiness. That to secure these rights Governments are instituted among Men, deriving their just powers from the consent of the Governed. That whenever any form of the Government becomes destructive of these ends, it is the right of the People to alter or abolish it and to institute new Government....". This Declaration of Independence by and for the people of a new American Nation still has global implications. The same can be said about the Declaration of the Rights of Man and the Citizen issued by France's National Assembly in 1789, which proclaimed: "The end of all political associations is the preservation of natural and imprescriptible rights of man; and these rights are liberty, property, security, and resistance of oppression".

The 1787 Constitution and the 1791 Bill of Rights of the United States of America were designed and adopted to address the Civic values of the 1776 Declaration of Independence. This Constitution reflects the understanding among America's founders that the individual's rights are at risk if government is either too strong or too weak. A good government simultaneously is empowered and limited. It is empowered sufficiently by the people to secure their rights against domestic or foreign predators. And this government's powers are also limited sufficiently by the supreme law of its Constitution to protect the people's rights against abuses by their own governors.

During the nineteenth and twentieth centuries, the concept of Natural Rights was transformed into the idea of Human Rights. This change reflected an expansion of the scope or range of rights to include two types of claims.

The first and older type is negative; it would limit the power of the government to protect people's rights against its power. The second and newer type of claim is positive; it would enhance the power of the government to do something for the person to enable her or him in some way. Thus, the late twentieth century idea of human rights, which incorporates both the positive and negative types, means that "certain things ought not to be done to any human being and certain other things ought to be done for every human being".

The older negative claims on rights are exemplified by

Articles 1-21 of the United Nations Universal Declaration of Human Rights. These Articles imply that no government or society should act against individuals in certain ways that would deprive them of inherent political or personal rights, such as freedom of speech, press, assembly, and religion. The newer positive claims on rights are exemplified by Articles 22-28 of the Universal Declaration of Human Rights. They imply that every government and every society should act for individual members to enable them to enjoy certain social and economic rights or benefits pertaining to social security, employment, housing, education, health care and general standard of living. In International discourse, the problem of rights is often posed as a series of oppositional dichotomies: *Universalism V. Cultural* Relativism; the *Individual V. Collective*; *Civil and Political V. Economic, Social and Cultural*, behind these dichotomies are real ones that need to be addressed carefully by the human rights community. At the same time our world is increasingly, and irrevocably, international: in economics, politics, and communications, we are all now bound to each other through complicated webs of dependence, infiltration and, most painfully, inequality and domination. In such a world, human rights affirms the basic entitlement of all people to resources and to the respect and dignity that comes from the ability to consciously, willfully participate in setting the terms of their interactions with the world around them.

No one fools themselves into believing that we are close to such an ideal. No one fools themselves into thinking that its attainment will be easy or that it will come without massive social change, in which some will be required to relinquish power over others. But in the area of health, in which we can see in the most obvious physical terms the results of structures of inequality large and small, we have perhaps the best chance to make a difference, to determine and implement, social configurations that can support and promote human well-being. In short, when human rights principles are applied to health, we begin to have strategic, political basis upon which to mobilize across the divides of nation, culture, class, race, and religion, in support of each other and in pursuit of change.

Health is a fundamental human right indispensable for the exercise of other human rights. Every human being is entitled to the enjoyment of the highest attainable standard of health conducive to living a life in dignity. The realization of the Right to Health may be pursued through numerous, complementary approaches, such as formulation of health policies, or the implementation of health programmes developed by the World Health Organisation (WHO), or the adoption of specific legal instruments. Moreover, the Right to Health includes certain components which are legally enforceable.

The human Right to Health is recognised in numerous international instruments. Article 25.1 of the Universal Declaration of Human Rights affirms: "Everyone has the right to a standard of living adequate, for the health of himself and of his family, including food, clothing, housing and medical care and necessary social services". The International Covenant on Economic, Social and Cultural Rights provides the most comprehensive article on the right to health in international human rights law. In accordance with Article 12.1 of the Covenant, State Parties recognise "the right of everyone to the enjoyment of the highest attainable standard of physical and mental health", while Article 12.2 enumerates, by way of illustration, a number of "steps to be taken by the State Parties... to achieve the full realization of this right". Additionally, the Right to Health is recognised, *inter alia*, in Article 5(e)(iv) of the International Convention on the Elimination of All forms of Racial Discrimination of 1965, in Articles 11.1(f) and 12 of the Convention on the Elimination of All forms of Discrimination Against Women of 1979 and in Article 24 of the Convention on the Rights of the Child of 1989. Several regional human rights instruments also recognise the Right to Health, such as European Social Charter of 1961 as revised (Article 11), the African Charter on Human and Peoples' Rights in the area of Economic, Social and Cultural Rights of 1988 (Article 10). Similarly, the Right to Health has been proclaimed by the Commission on Human Rights (Resolution 1989/11.) as well as in the Vienna Declaration and Programme of Action of 1993 and other international instruments.

The Right to Health is closely related to and dependent upon the realization of other human rights, as contained in the International Bill of Rights, including the rights to food, housing, work, education, human dignity, life, non-discrimination, equality, privacy, access to information... These and other rights and freedoms address integral components of the Right to Health. In drafting Article 12 of the Covenant, the Third Committee of the United Nations General Assembly did not adopt the definition of health contained in the Preamble to the Constitution of WHO, which conceptualizes health as "a state of complete physical, mental and social well-being and not merely the absence of disease and infirmity". However, the reference in Article 12.1 of the Covenant to "the highest attainable standard of physical and mental health" is not confined to the Right to Health care. On the contrary, the drafting history and the express wording of Article 12.2 acknowledge that the Right to Health embraces a wide range of socio-economic factors that promote conditions in which people can lead a healthy life, and extends to the underlying determinants of health, such as food, nutrition, housing, access to safe and potable water and adequate sanitation, safe and healthy environment.

Everyone likes to live in a healthy environment which is basic human right (necessity). Healthy environment is a nature's gift. Air and water are essential for living things. In 1968 the UN General Assembly passed a Resolution identifying the relationship between the quality of human environment and the enjoyment of basic rights. This was followed by the landmark Stockholm Declaration in June 1972 to which India was a party, is called The Magna Carta of our Environment, which stated that "both aspects of man's environment, the natural and man-made are essential to the well-being and to the enjoyment of basic-rights even the Right to Life itself", and that man has the Fundamental Right to freedom, equality and adequate conditions of life, in an environment quality that permits a life of dignity and well being...". More recently the Hague Declaration stated that "the Right to Life is the paramount duty of those in charge of all States throughout the world". In 1990 the UN General Assembly declared that "all individuals are entitled to live in an environment adequate for their health and well-being". The United Nations Commission on Human Rights also adopted a Resolution in 1990, entitled "Human Rights and the Environment", which again reaffirmed the relationship between preservation of environment and the promotion of human rights. Eventually in 1992 the Rio Declaration relates the rights issue to the broader issue of sustainable development. This is expressed in Principle 1 : "human beings are at the centre of concerns for sustainable development. They are entitled to healthy and productive life in harmony with nature".

Environmental deterioration could eventually endanger life of present and future generations. Therefore, the Right to Life has been used in a diversified manner in India. It includes, *inter alia*, the right to survive as a species, quality of life, the right to live with dignity and the right to livelihood. Article 21 of the Constitution of India states: "No person shall be deprived of his life or personal liberty except according to procedure established by law. The Supreme Court expanded this negative right in two ways. Firstly, any law affecting personal liberty should be reasonable, fair and just. Secondly, the Court recognised several un-articulated liberties that were implied by article 21. It is by this second method that the Supreme Court interpreted the Right to Life and Personal Liberty to include the Right to a Clean Environment.

In addition, the Constitution (Forty Second Amendment) Act, 1976 explicitly incorporated environmental protection and improvement as a part of State Policy, Article 48-A, a Directive

Principle of State Policy, provides that: 'The State shall endeavour to protect and improve the environment and safeguard the forests and wildlife of the country'. Moreover, Article 51A(g) imposes a similar responsibility on every citizen to protect and improve the natural environment including forests, lakes, rivers and wildlife, and to have a compassion for living creatures....' Together, these Articles, highlight the national consensus on the importance of the protection and improvement of the environment.

Under prevailing deteriorating environmental conditions need of the hour is that different cross sections of the society have to voice their concern on degradation of environment at different fora. It would be interesting to examine as to whose concern is environment. Some of the major players involved are elected representatives, bureaucrats, technocrats, NGOs and judiciary. The elected representatives are often in a hurry to show their achievements in the form of some developmental projects especially in their respective constituencies. Often bureaucrats are under pressure from political bosses as well as from public. As a result they try to perform a balancing act and at times follow the path of least resistance. Some of the technocrats in the environmental protection and pollution control authorities, who take their jobs Seriously and sincerely and act in accordance with the '*spirit and letter*' of the concerned acts and notifications, are often considered as stumbling blocks to the economic development and are branded as anti-development. Multilateral funding agencies insist on the involvement of the NGOs in almost every walk of life. Can all NGOs be considered as self-styled protectors of environment ? Whereas there are some genuine NGOs who are committed to the cause but this may not be true for all the NGOs. There appears no accountability of NGOs under the present set of regulations.

Indiscipline is prevalent among industries that have by and large, consider air, water and land as free and unlimited common property. Thus the *onus* lies on governmental agencies to design suitable framework of policy formulation, effective monitoring and mechanism of punishing defaulters.

In the industrially advanced countries, the public and NGOs have reached a level of awareness whereby purchase of green products, purchase form green producers and boycott of polluters is practiced in daily life. In a developing country like ours the response of public and NGOs has been little different. Sooner or later such a high level of awareness is bound to reach in our public also. Thus industry has got limited time to implement green productivity by discontinuing the production and usage of hazardous or toxic substances, reducing discharges and emissions into the atmosphere and increasing efficiencies of conversion of raw materials and energy. Various case studies have revealed that there is a strong correlation between environmental degradation and chronic poverty in developing and under developed economies. New tools for decision-making including remote sensing are available which can indicate the changes in the land use pattern, degradation of soils and changes in the water resources. The principle of sustainable development can not be considered as pessimistic. However, the concerns need to be addressed in a cautious way. Thus the paradigm is sustainable development, which includes the concern on resources, socio-economic aspects and also the ecology.

The process of transfer of internationally proven technology in this field has to be considered on a separate footing, considering its impact on humanity as a whole. Mandated emission levels, which can be achieved only by application of specific technologies, automatically confer monopolistic powers on the holders of the technology and enable them to earn unjustified rent. This is iniquitous. Since the environment is of concern to all, there is no justification for some to earn large rents at the cost of the vast majority. Fair return of technological development must of course be there, but nothing beyond. The Global Environmental Fund (GEF) attempts to tackle this issue in part, but a partial reimbursement is not a corrective for the essential distortion. Mechanisms need to evolved to be ensure both the development of technologies and their dissemination at fair non-distorting prices. This is a case for transferring these technologies at variable incentive prices to countries with the highest potential for controlling damaging emissions.

Research and Development can play a crucial role in the protection of environment. Only the need is the commitment of policy makers, environmental professionals, industrialists, researchers and NGOs under a common roof.

The awareness regarding health and environment, which has been created since the Rio Declaration in 1992, should be used as an opportunity to place health at the centre of development, create an enabling/supportive environment for health and for sustainable development. In this regard education is an important tool to change the rules of the game of life. Persons who are educated develop physically (economically), mentally, emotionally, morally and socially. They are likely to know the whys and the wherefores of events and issues surrounding them. Their uncertainties about many things in life, if not about life itself, are reduced. At least they try to understand them and remove their ignorance, uncertainties and fear. They can map their world, their immediate environment and live a more meaningful life.

Many of our problems could be avoided if we follow the preaching of Indian culture. It may be recalled that our culture has given lot of importance to Panchbhuta viz. water, air, land, energy and space, which is nothing but environment. A number of mantras in Vedas deal about the potentiality of individual and ultimate concept of the energy (shakti) and directs the people on earth to pray and worship them for a balanced and harmonious approach of environment. In Vedic Dharma the human life and the environment are inseparable. Therefore, all lives, human and non-human, are of equal value, and have same right to existence.

Further Shanti Mantras of Rig Veda attest to the belief that life either of man or of animal can prevail only when the entire environment and cosmos prevails in peace. So the life of the man which is considered to be decent livable life depends entirely on the total state of the environment. That is why protection of the environment from pollution becomes an imperative duty.

To quote Ishopanishad - one of the oldest Hindu religious philosophical text : "All, in this manifested world, consisting of moving and non-moving, are covered by the Lord. Use its resources with restraint. Do not grab the property of others distant and yet to come". Similarly the Holy Quran mentions in [54:49] "Indeed we have created everything in proportion and due measure" and in [7:31] it is said : eat and drink, but waste not by excess. For Allah loveth not the wasters. The Holy Quran is clear on this point : "And do not make mischief on Earth after it has been set in order..." [7:56]. Any disorder leading to the pollution, deterioration or harmful alteration of the environment is considered in Islam as Fasad (mischief). Thus spirit of Vasudhava Kutumbakam of love thy neighbour, peaceful co-existence of all living beings, and respect for nature, if practiced by all of us religiously, would indeed make our planet worth living for all the times to come.

Appendices

Draft Declaration of Principles on Human Rights and the Environment, 1994

HUMAN RIGHTS AND THE ENVIRONMENT

On 16 May 1994, an international group of experts on human rights and environmental protection convened at the United Nations in Geneva and drafted the first-ever declaration of principles on human rights and the environment.

The Geneva group assembled at the invitation of the Sierra Club Legal Defense Fund—in cooperation with the Association mondiale pour l'cole instrument de paix and the Socit suisse pour la protection de l'environnement- -on behalf of Madame Fatma Zohra Ksentini, Special Rapporteur on Human Rights and the Environment for the United Nations Sub-Commission on Prevention of Discrimination and Protection of Minorities.

As U.N. Special Rapporteur, Madame Ksentini has since 1989 presided over a study of the connections between human rights and the environment. Madame Ksentini's final report to the Sub-Commission is due in August 1994. The final report will include the Draft Declaration produced at the Geneva Meeting of Experts.

The Draft Declaration is the first international instrument that comprehensively addresses the linkage between human rights and the environment. It demonstrates that accepted environmental and human rights principles embody the right of everyone to a secure, healthy and ecologically sound environment. The Draft Declaration describes the environmental dimension of established human rights, such as the rights to life, health and culture. It also describes the procedural rights, such as the right to participation, necessary for realization of the substantive rights.

The Draft Declaration also describes duties that correspond to the rights—duties that apply to individuals, governments, international organizations and transnational corporations.

DRAFT DECLARATION OF PRINCIPLES ON HUMAN RIGHTS AND THE ENVIRONMENT

Preamble

Guided by the United Nations Charter, the Universal Declaration of Human Rights, the International Covenant on Economic, Social and Cultural Rights, the International Covenant on Civil and Political Rights, the Vienna Declaration and Program of Action of the World Conference of Human Rights, and other relevant international human rights instruments,

Guided also by the Stockholm Declaration of the United Nations Conference on the Human Environment, the World Charter for Nature, the Rio Declaration on Environment and Development, Agenda 21: Programme of Action for Sustainable Development, and other relevant instruments of international environmental law,

Guided also by the Declaration on the Right to Development, which recognizes that the right to development is an essential human right and that the human person is the central subject of development,

Guided further by fundamental principles of international humanitarian law, Reaffirming the universality, indivisibility and interdependence of all human rights, Recognizing that sustainable development links the right to development and the right to a secure, healthy and ecologically sound environment, Recalling the right of peoples to self-determination, by virtue of which they have the right freely to determine their political status and to pursue their economic, social and cultural development,

Deeply concerned by the severe human rights consequences of environmental harm caused by poverty, structural adjustment and debt programmes and by international trade and intellectual property regimes,

Convinced that the potential irreversibility of environmental harm gives rise to special responsibility to prevent such harm,

Concerned that human rights violations lead to environmental degradation and that environmental degradation leads to human rights violations,

THE FOLLOWING PRINCIPLES ARE DECLARED

Part I

1. Human rights, an ecologically sound environment, sustainable development and peace are interdependent and indivisible.
2. All persons have the right to a secure, healthy and ecologically sound environment. This right and other human rights, including civil, cultural, economic, political and social rights, are universal, interdependent and indivisible.
3. All persons shall be free from any form of discrimination in regard to actions and decisions that affect the environment.
4. All persons have the right to an environment adequate to meet equitably the needs of present generations and that does not impair the rights of future generations to meet equitably their needs.

Part II

5. All persons have the right to freedom from pollution, environmental degradation and activities that adversely

affect the environment, threaten life, health, livelihood, well-being or sustainable development within, across or outside national boundaries.

6. All persons have the right to protection and preservation of the air, soil, water, sea-ice, flora and fauna, and the essential processes and areas necessary to maintain biological diversity and ecosystems.
7. All persons have the right to the highest attainable standard of health free from environmental pollution.
8. All persons have the right to safe and healthy food and water adequate to their well-being.
9. All persons have the right to a safe and healthy working environment.
10. All persons have the right to adequate housing, land tenure and living conditions in a secure, healthy and ecologically sound environment.
11. All persons have the right not to be evicted from their homes or land for the purpose of, or as a consequence of, decisions or actions affecting the environment, except in emergencies or due to a compelling purpose benefiting society as a whole and not attainable by other means. All persons have the right to participate effectively in decisions and to negotiate concerning their eviction and the right, if evicted, to timely and adequate restitution, compensation and/or appropriate and sufficient accommodation or land.
12. All persons have the right to timely assistance in the event of natural or technological or other human-caused catastrophes.
13. Everyone has the right to benefit equitably from the conservation and sustainable use of nature and natural resources for cultural, ecological, educational, health, livelihood, recreational, spiritual or other purposes. This includes ecologically sound access to nature.

Everyone has the right to preservation of unique sites, consistent with the fundamental rights of persons or groups living in the area.

14. Indigenous peoples have the right to control their lands, territories and natural resources and to maintain their traditional way of life. This includes the right to security in the enjoyment of their means of subsistence.

    Indigenous peoples have the right to protection against any action or course of conduct that may result in the destruction or degradation of their territories, including land, air, water, sea-ice, wildlife or other resources.

Part III

15. All persons have the right to information concerning the environment. This includes information, howsoever compiled, on actions and courses of conduct that may affect the environment and information necessary to enable effective public participation in environmental decision-making. The information shall be timely, clear, understandable and available without undue financial burden to the applicant.
16. All persons have the right to hold and express opinions and to disseminate ideas and information regarding the environment.
17. All persons have the right to environmental and human rights education.
18. All persons have the right to active, free, and meaningful participation in planning and decision-making activities and processes that may have an impact on the environment and development. This includes the right to a prior assessment of the environmental, developmental and human rights consequences of proposed actions.
19. All persons have the right to associate freely and peacefully with others for purposes of protecting the environment or the rights of persons affected by environmental harm.

20. All persons have the right to effective remedies and redress in administrative or judicial proceedings for environmental harm or the threat of such harm.

Part IV

21. All persons, individually and in association with others, have a duty to protect and preserve the environment.

22. All States shall respect and ensure the right to a secure, healthy and ecologically sound environment. Accordingly, they shall adopt the administrative, legislative and other measures necessary to effectively implement the rights in this Declaration.

These measures shall aim at the prevention of environmental harm, at the provision of adequate remedies, and at the sustainable use of natural resources and shall include, inter alia, collection and dissemination of information concerning the environment prior assessment and control, licensing, regulation or prohibition of activities and substances potentially harmful to the environment; public participation in environmental decision-making; effective administrative and judicial remedies and redress for environmental harm and the threat of such harm; monitoring, management and equitable sharing of natural resources; measures to reduce wasteful processes of production and patterns of consumption; measures aimed at ensuring that transnational corporations, wherever they operate, carry out their duties of environmental protection, sustainable development and respect for human rights; and measures aimed at ensuring that the international organizations and agencies to which they belong observe the rights and duties in this Declaration.

23. States and all other parties shall avoid using the environment as a means of war or inflicting significant, long-term or widespread harm on the environment, and shall respect international law providing protection for the environment in times of armed conflict and cooperate in its further development.

24. All international organizations and agencies shall observe the rights and duties in this Declaration.

Part V

25. In implementing the rights and duties in this Declaration, special attention shall be given to vulnerable persons and groups.

26. The rights in this Declaration may be subject only to restrictions provided by law and which are necessary to protect public order, health and the fundamental rights and freedoms of others.

27. All persons are entitled to a social and international order in which the rights in this Declaration can be fully realized.

Declaration of the United Nations Conference on the Human Environment, 1972

The United Nations Conference on the Human Environment, Having met at Stockholm *from 5 to 16 June 1972*, *Having considered* the need for a common outlook and for common principles to inspire and guide the peoples of the world in the preservation and enhancement of the human environment,

I

Proclaims that:

1. Man is both creature and moulder of the environment, which gives him physical sustenance and affords him the opportunity for intellectual, moral, social and spiritual growth. In the long and tortuous evolution of the human race on this planet a stage has been reached when, through the rapid acceleration of science and technology, man has acquired the power to transform his environment in countless ways and on an unprecedented scale. Both aspects of man's environment, the natural and the man-made, are essential to his well-being and to the enjoyment of basic human rights - even the right to life itself.
2. The protection and improvement of the human environment is a major issue which affects the well being of peoples and economic development throughout the world; it is the urgent desire of the peoples of the whole world and the duty of all Governments.

3. Man has constantly to sum up experience and go on discovering, inventing, creating and advancing. In our time, man's capability to transform his surroundings, if used wisely, can bring to all peoples the benefits of development and the opportunity to enhance the quality of life. Wrongly or heedlessly applied, the same power can do incalculable harm to human beings and the human environment. We see around us growing evidence of man-made harm in many regions of the earth: dangerous levels of pollution in water, air, earth and living beings; major and undesirable disturbances to the ecological balance of the biosphere; destruction and depletion of irreplaceable resources; and gross deficiencies harmful to the physical, mental and social health of man, in the man-made environment, particularly in the living and working environment.

4. In the developing countries most of the environmental problems are caused by under-development. Millions continue to live far below the minimum levels required for a decent human existence, deprived of adequate food and clothing, shelter and education, health and sanitation. Therefore, the developing countries must direct their efforts to development, bearing in mind their priorities and the need to safeguard and improve the environment. For the same purpose, the industrialized countries should make efforts to reduce the gap between themselves and the developing countries. In the industrialized countries, environmental problems are generally related to industrialization and technological development.

5. The natural growth of population continuously presents problems on the preservation of the environment, and adequate policies and measures should be adopted, as appropriate, to face these problems. Of all things in the world, people are the most precious. It is the people that propel social progress, create social wealth, develop science and technology and, through their hard work,

continuously transform the human environment. Along with social progress and the advance of production, science and technology, the capability of man to improve the environment increases with each passing day.

6. A point has been reached in history when we must shape our actions throughout the world with a more prudent care for their environmental consequences. Through ignorance or indifference we can do massive and irreversible harm to the early environment on which our life and well-being depend. Conversely, through fuller knowledge and wiser action, we can achieve for ourselves and our posterity a better life in an environment more in keeping with human needs and hopes. There are broad vistas for the enhancement of environmental quality and the creation of a good life. What is needed is an enthusiastic but calm state of mind and intense but orderly work. For the purpose of attaining freedom in the world of nature, man must use knowledge to build, in collaboration with nature, a better environment. To defend and improve the human environment for present and future generations has become an imperative goal for mankind a goal to be pursued together with, and in harmony with, the established and fundamental goals of peace and of world-wide economic and social development.

7. To achieve this environmental goal will demand the acceptance of responsibility by citizens and communities and by enterprises and institutions at every level, all sharing equitably in common efforts. Individuals in all walks of life as well as organizations in many fields, by their values and the sum of their actions, will shape the world environment of the future. Local and national governments will bear the greatest burden for large-scale environmental policy and action within their jurisdictions. International co-operation is also needed in order to raise resources to support the developing countries in carrying out their

responsibilities in this field. A growing class of environmental problems, because they are regional or global in extent or because they affect the common international realm, will require extensive co-operation among nations and action by international organizations in the common interest. The Conference calls upon Governments and peoples to exert common efforts for the preservation and improvement of the human environment, for the benefit of all the people and for their posterity.

II

Principles

States of common conviction that:

Principle 1

Man has the fundamental right to freedom, equality and adequate conditions of life, in an environment of a quality that permits a life of dignity and well-being; and he bears a solemn responsibility to protect and improve the environment for present and future generations. In this respect, policies promoting or perpetuating apartheid, racial segregation, discrimination, colonial and other forms of oppression and foreign domination stand condemned and must be eliminated.

Principle 2

The natural resources of the earth including the air, water, land, flora and fauna and especially representative samples of natural ecosystems must be safeguard for the benefit of present and future generations through careful planning or management, as appropriate.

Principle 3

The capacity of the earth to produce vital renewable resources must be maintained and, wherever practicable, restored or improved.

Principle 4

Man has a special responsibility to safeguard and wisely manage the heritage of wildlife and its habitat which are now gravely imperilled by a combination of adverse factors. Nature conservation including wildlife must therefore receive importance in planning for economic development.

Principle 5

The non-renewable resources of the earth must be employed in a way as to guard against the danger of their future exhaustion and to ensure that benefits from such employment are shared by all mankind.

Principle 6

The discharge of toxic substances or of other substances and the release of heat, in such quantities or concentrations as to exceed the capacity of the environment to render them harmless, must be halted in order to ensure that serious or irreversible damage is not inflicted upon ecosystems. The just struggle of the peoples of all countries against pollution should be supported.

Principle 7

States shall take all possible steps to prevent pollution of the seas by substances that are liable to create hazards to human health, to harm living resources and marine life, to damage amenities or to interfere with other legitimate uses of the sea.

Principle 8

Economic and social development is essential for ensuring a favourable living and working environment for man and for creating conditions on earth that are necessary for the improvement of the quality of life.

Principle 9

Environmental deficiencies generated by the conditions of underdevelopment and natural disasters pose grave problems and can best be remedied by accelerated development through the transfer of substantial quantities of financial and technological assistance as a supplement to the domestic effort of the developing countries and such timely assistance as may be required.

Principle 10

For the developing countries, stability of prices and adequate earnings for primary commodities and raw material are essential to environmental management since economic factors as well as ecological processes must be taken into account.

Principle 11

The environmental policies of all States should enhance and not adversely affect the present or future development potential of developing countries, nor should they hamper the attainment of better living conditions for all, and appropriate steps should be taken by States and international organizations with a view to reaching agreement on meeting the possible national and international economic consequences resulting from the application of environmental measures.

Principle 12

Resources should be made available to preserve and improve the environment, taking into account the circumstances and particular requirements of developing countries and any costs which may emanate from their incorporating environmental safeguards into their development planning and the need for making available to them, upon their request, additional international technical and financial assistance for this purpose.

Principle 13

In order to achieve a more rational management of resources and thus to improve the environment, States should adopt an integrated and co-ordinated approach to their development planning so as to ensure that development is compatiable with the need to protect and improve the human environment for the benefit of their population.

Principle 14

Rational planning constitutes an essential tool of reconciling any conflict between the needs of development and the need to protect and improve the environment.

Principle 15

Planning must be applied to human settlements and urbanization with a view to avoiding adverse effects on the environment and obtaining maximum social, economic and environmental benefits for all. In this respect projects which are designed for colonialist and racist domination must be abandoned.

Principle 16

Demographic policies, which are without prejudice to basic human rights and which are deemed appropriate by Governments concerned, should be applied in those regions where the rate of population growth or excessive population concentrations are likely to have adverse effects on the environment or development, or where low population density may prevent improvement of the human environment and impede development.

Principle 17

Appropriate national institutions must be entrusted with the task of planning, managing or controlling the environmental resources of States with the view to enhancing environmental quality.

Principle 18

Science and technology, as part of their contribution to economic and social development, must be applied to the identification, avoidance and control of environment risks and the solution of environmental problems and for the common good of mankind.

Principle 19

Education in environmental matters, for the younger generation as well as adults, giving due consideration to the underprivileged, is essential in order to broaden the basis for an enlightened opinion and responsible conduct by individuals, enterprises and communities in protecting and improving the environment in its full human dimension. It is also essential that mass media of communications avoid contributing to the deterioration of the environment, but, on the contrary, disseminate information of an educational nature, on the need to protect and improve the environment in order to enable man to develop in every respect.

Principle 20

Scientific research and development in the context of environmental problems, both national and multinational, must be promoted in all countries, especially the developing countries. In the connexion, the free flow of up-to-date scientific information and transfer of experience must be supported and assisted, to facilitate the solution of environmental problems; environmental technologies should be made available to developing countries on terms which would encourage their wide dissemination without constituting an economic burden on the developing countries.

Principle 21

States have, in accordance with the Charter of the United Nations and the principle of international law, the sovereign right to exploit their own resources pursuant to their own environmental policies, and the responsibility to ensure that activities within their jurisdiction or control do not cause damage to the environment of other States or of areas beyond the limits of national jurisdiction.

Principle 22

States shall co-operate to develop further the international law regarding liability and compensation for the victims of pollution and other environmental damage caused by activities within the jurisdiction or control of such States to areas beyond their jurisdiction.

Principle 23

Without prejudice to such criteria as may be agreed upon by the international community, or to standards which will have to be determined nationally, it will be essential in all cases to consider the systems of values prevailing in each country and the extent of the applicability of standards which are valid for the most advanced countries but which may be inappropriate and of unwarranted social cost for the developing countries.

Principle 24

International matters concerning the protection and improvement of the environment should be handled in a co-operative spirit by all countries, big or small, on an equal footing. Co-operation through multilateral or bilateral arrangements or other appropriate means is essential to effectively control, prevent, reduce and eliminate adverse environmental effects resulting from activities conducted in all spheres, in such a way that due account is taken of the sovereignty and interests of all States.

Principle 25

State shall ensure that international organizations play a co-ordinated, efficient and dynamic role for the protection and improvement of the environment.

Principle 26

Man and his environment must be spared the effects of nuclear weapons and all other means of mass destruction. States must strive to reach prompt agreement, in the relevant international organs, on the elimination and complete destruction of such weapons.

21st plenary meeting

16 June 1972

The Rio Declaration on Environment and Development (1992)

PREAMBLE

The United Nations Conference on Environment and Development, Having met at Rio de Janeiro from 3 to 14 June 1992, Reaffirming the Declaration of the United Nations Conference on the Human Environment, adopted at Stockholm on 16 June 1972, and seeking to build upon it,

With the goal of establishing a new and equitable global partnership through the creation of new levels of cooperation among States, key sectors of societies and people, Working towards international agreements which respect the interests of all and protect the integrity of the global environmental and developmental system, Recognizing the integral and interdependent nature of the Earth, our home,

PROCLAIMS THAT

Principle 1

Human beings are at the centre of concerns for sustainable development. They are entitled to a healthy and productive life in harmony with nature.

Principle 2

States have, in accordance with the Charter of the United Nations and the principles of international law, the sovereign right to exploit their own resources pursuant to their own environmental and developmental policies, and the responsibility to ensure that activities within their jurisdiction or control do not cause damage to the environment of other States or of areas beyond the limits of national jurisdiction.

Principle 3

The right to development must be fulfilled so as to equitably meet developmental and environmental needs of present and future generations.

Principle 4

In order to achieve sustainable development, environmental protection shall constitute an integral part of the development process and cannot be considered in isolation from it.

Principle 5

All States and all people shall cooperate in the essential task of eradicating poverty as an indispensable requirement for sustainable development, in order to decrease the disparities in standards of living and better meet the needs of the majority of the people of the world.

Principle 6

The special situation and needs of developing countries, particularly the least developed and those most environmentally vulnerable, shall be given special priority. International actions in the field of environment and development should also address the interests and needs of all countries.

Principle 7

States shall cooperate in a spirit of global partnership to conserve, protect and restore the health and integrity of the Earth's ecosystem. In view of the different contributions to global environmental degradation, States have common but differentiated responsibilities. The developed countries acknowledge the responsibility that they bear in the international pursuit of sustainable development in view of the pressures their societies place on the global environment and of the technologies and financial resources they command.

Principle 8

To achieve sustainable development and a higher quality of life for all people, States should reduce and eliminate unsustainable patterns of production and consumption and promote appropriate demographic policies.

Principle 9

States should cooperate to strengthen endogenous capacity-building for sustainable development by improving scientific understanding through exchanges of scientific and technological knowledge, and by enhancing the development, adaptation, diffusion and transfer of technologies, including new and innovative technologies.

Principle 10

Environmental issues are best handled with the participation of all concerned citizens, at the relevant level. At the national level, each individual shall have appropriate access to information concerning the environment that is held by public authorities, including information on hazardous materials and activities in their communities, and the opportunity to participate in decision-making processes. States shall facilitate and encourage public awareness and participation by making information widely available. Effective access to judicial and administrative proceedings, including redress and remedy, shall be provided.

Principle 11

States shall enact effective environmental legislation. Environmental standards, management objectives and priorities should reflect the environmental and developmental context to which they apply. Standards applied by some countries may be inappropriate and of unwarranted economic and social cost to other countries, in particular developing countries.

Principle 12

States should cooperate to promote a supportive and open

international economic system that would lead to economic growth and sustainable development in all countries, to better address the problems of environmental degradation. Trade policy measures for environmental purposes should not constitute a means of arbitrary or unjustifiable discrimination or a disguised restriction on international trade. Unilateral actions to deal with environmental challenges outside the jurisdiction of the importing country should be avoided. Environmental measures addressing transboundary or global environmental problems should, as far as possible, be based on an international consensus.

Principle 13

States shall develop national law regarding liability and compensation for the victims of pollution and other environmental damage. States shall also cooperate in an expeditious and more determined manner to develop further international law regarding liability and compensation for adverse effects of environmental damage caused by activities within their jurisdiction or control to areas beyond their jurisdiction.

Principle 14

States should effectively cooperate to discourage or prevent the relocation and transfer to other States of any activities and substances that cause severe environmental degradation or are found to be harmful to human health.

Principle 15

In order to protect the environment, the precautionary approach shall be widely applied by States according to their capabilities. Where there are threats of serious or irreversible damage, lack of full scientific certainty shall not be used as a reason for postponing cost-effective measures to prevent environmental degradation.

Principle 16

National authorities should endeavour to promote the internalization of environmental costs and the use of economic instruments, taking into account the approach that the polluter should, in principle, bear the cost of pollution, with due regard to the public interest and without distorting international trade and investment.

Principle 17

Environmental impact assessment, as a national instrument, shall be undertaken for proposed activities that are likely to have a significant adverse impact on the environment and are subject to a decision of a competent national authority.

Principle 18

States shall immediately notify other States of any natural disasters or other emergencies that are likely to produce sudden harmful effects on the environment of those States. Every effort shall be made by the international community to help States so afflicted.

Principle 19

States shall provide prior and timely notification and relevant information to potentially affected States on activities that may have a significant adverse transboundary environmental effect and shall consult with those States at an early stage and in good faith.

Principle 20

Women have a vital role in environmental management and development. Their full participation is therefore essential to achieve sustainable development.

Principle 21

The creativity, ideals and courage of the youth of the world should be mobilized to forge a global partnership in order to achieve sustainable development and ensure a better future for all.

Principle 22

Indigenous people and their communities, and other local

communities, have a vital role in environmental management and development because of their knowledge and traditional practices. States should recognize and duly support their identity, culture and interests and enable their effective participation in the achievement of sustainable development.

Principle 23

The environment and natural resources of people under oppression, domination and occupation shall be protected.

Principle 24

Warfare is inherently destructive of sustainable development. States shall therefore respect international law providing protection for the environment in times of armed conflict and cooperate in its further development, as necessary.

Principle 25

Peace, development and environmental protection are interdependent and indivisible.

Principle 26

States shall resolve all their environmental disputes peacefully and by appropriate means in accordance with the Charter of the United Nations.

Principle 27

States and people shall cooperate in good faith and in a spirit of partnership in the fulfilment of the principles embodied in this Declaration and in the further development of international law in the field of sustainable development.

AGENDA 21: A SUMMARY

The United Nations Conference on Environment and Development (UNCED), also called the Earth Summit, took place in Rio de Janeiro, Brazil, in June 1992. This largest-ever world meeting brought Heads of State and government officials together with international organizations and representatives of non-government organizations (NGOs) from around the world.

A 700 page global plan of action called Agenda 21 was produced as a result of the Earth Summit: it represents the consensus reached by 178 States on how we can secure OUR future. Agenda 21 is like a blueprint (or maybe we should call it a "green print"!) for global partnership aiming at a high quality environment and a healthy economy for all peoples of the planet.

Agenda 21 addresses the critical issues we face as a global community: continuing damage to ecosystems, the worsening of poverty, hunger and ill health, increasing world population and illiteracy. Agenda 21 is composed of 40 chapters that identify each challenge and propose simple realistic solutions towards sustainable development which is: meeting the needs of the present without compromising the ability of future generations to meet their own needs.

Around the world, governments, businesses, non-governmental and other organizations are already putting the ideas from Agenda 21 to work. It is crucial to maintain the momentum of the Rio process and implement the agreements that were reached. This task will require not only the leadership and funding of governments and business, but also the vision, cooperation and work of every citizen. Sustainable development cannot be achieved without all sectors of society working together.

PART ONE- LINKING SOCIETY, ECONOMY AND NATURE

This section focuses on the importance of international cooperation to implement and speed up our progress toward sustainable development. It stresses the necessity for the governments of each individual developed and developing country to implement new policies, laws and strategies aimed at socially responsible development. However, governments cannot do it alone, they will need to work with the private sector, non-governmental organizations and individuals.

Chapter 1

Preamble to Agenda 21: No nation can secure its future alone, but all countries can assure themselves of a safer, more prosperous future by dealing with environment and development issues TOGETHER in global partnership.

Chapter 2

The Role of TRADE: Trade and environment should be mutually supportive since international economic relations and the economic policies of every country have great relevance to sustainable development.

Chapter 3

Combating POVERTY: Poverty is caused by hunger, illiteracy, inadequate medical care, unemployment and population pressures. The poor need access to basic education and health care, safe water and sanitation, and to resources, especially land.

Chapter 4

Changing CONSUMPTION PATTERNS: New concepts of wealth and prosperity which are more in harmony with the Earth's carrying capacity need to be developed, particularly in the industrialized countries. Individuals need to accept that they have choices when making decisions about their own consumption patterns.

Chapter 5

POPULATION Dynamics: The world's population is expected to exceed 8 billion by the year 2020. Countries need to know their national population carrying capacity and deal with the combination of population growth, health of the ecosystem, technologies and access to resources.

Chapter 6

Protecting and Promoting HEALTH: Every year in the developing world, nearly 15 million children under 15 die from infection and malnutrition. Human health depends on a healthy environment, clean water supply, sanitary waste disposal, adequate shelter and healthy food. The overall goal is health for all by the year 2000.

Chapter 7

Sustainable Human settlements: By the year 2000, half the world's population will be living in cities. Governments should reduce migration to the big cities by improving rural living and see that the homeless get access to land, credit and low-cost building materials.

Chapter 8

MAKING DECISIONS for Sustainable Development: There is a tendency to treat the environment as a "free good" and to pass the cost of environmental damage to other parts of society, other countries or future generations. Nations and corporate enterprises should integrate environmental protection and restoration costs in their decision-making.

PART TWO-HOW CAN WE PROTECT OUR RESOURCES

Chapter 9

Protecting the ATMOSPHERE: Our atmosphere is under increasing pressure from greenhouse gases that threaten to change the climates and chemicals that reduce the ozone layer. Greater energy efficiency out of existing power stations is needed as well as developing new, renewable energy sources such as solar, wind, hydro, ocean and human power, while reducing reliance on non-renewable sources of energy such as fossil fuels.

Chapter 10

Planning and Management of LAND-USE: Increasing demand for land and its natural resources is creating competition and conflicts. Sustainable use and management of land should include landscape ecological planning, traditional and indigenous land practices and the active participation in decision-making by people affected by land planning.

Chapter 11

Combating DEFORESTATION: There is a need for concerted international research and conservation efforts to control the harvesting of forests by promoting indigenous technologies and agro forestry and expanding the shrunken world-forest cover.

Chapter 12

Combating DESERTIFICATION: Desertification and drought result in poverty and starvation, which brings about more soil degradation. One of the major tools to fight the spread of deserts is the planting of trees and other plants that retain water and maintain soil quality.

Chapter 13

MOUNTAIN Development: About 10% of the Earth's population live in mountain areas, while about 40% occupies watershed areas below. Measures are needed to protect mountain ecosystems from erosion, landslides and the rapid loss of habitat, animals and plant life.

Chapter 14

AGRICULTURE and Rural Development: The world's long-term ability to meet the growing demand for food and other agricultural products is uncertain. The priority must be to maintain and improve the capacity of agricultural lands with new technologies to support an expanding population.

Chapter 15

Conservation of BIODIVERSITY: The use of biological resources to feed and clothe us, to provide us with housing and medicines accelerates the loss of bio-diversity. Urgent and decisive action is needed to conserve and maintain genes, species and ecosystems.

Chapter 16

Sustainable BIOTECHNOLOGY: The success of

biotechnology programs depends on highly trained scientific professionals who use traditional knowledge and modern technology to change the genetic material in plants, animals and microbes and create new products such as vaccines, increase soil fertility and crop resistance, improve treatment of sewage, etc.

Chapter 17

Protection of the OCEANS: Oceans are under increasing stress from pollution, over-fishing and general degradation. Nations must control and reduce the pollution of the marine environment and maintain its life support capacity.

Chapter 18

Protecting and Managing WATER: In the developing world, one person in three lacks safe drinking water and sanitation p; basic requirements for health and dignity. A cleanup of the most obvious sources of pollution is needed in order to have safe water and sanitation for all by the year 2025.

Chapter 19

· **Management of TOXIC CHEMICALS:** There are presently no less than 100,000 commercial man-made chemicals. Countries need to develop and share expertise for a sound management of toxic chemicals and prevent illegal international traffic in toxic and dangerous products.

Chapter 20

HAZARDOUS WASTES: Developing countries have come under pressure to accept unpleasant imports of hazardous waste which pose a risk to people and the environment. Developed countries have an obligation to promote the transfer of sound technologies and reduce hazardous waste.

Chapter 21

SOLID WASTE and SEWAGE: Growing quantities of garbage and sewage from our cities pose threats to our health and environment. An urban waste prevention approach needs to be implemented so that by 2010, all countries should have national plans for waste management.

Chapter 22

RADIOACTIVE WASTE: The use of radioactive substances is growing in nuclear power production of electricity, medicine, research and industry and so is the waste. It is important to ensure training and financial support to developing countries that have nuclear programs to ensure safe and responsible management.

PART THREE- WHO CAN MAKE A DIFFERENCE

Chapter 23

Preamble: Sustainable development is primarily the responsibility of every government, but the commitment and involvement of all social groups is critical to the effective implementation of the objectives, policies and mechanisms agreed to by all governments at the Earth's Summit.

Chapter 24

WOMEN: Governments are urged to give girls equal access to education, to make health-care systems responsive to women's needs and to bring women into full participation in social, cultural and public life.

Chapter 25

CHILDREN and YOUTH: Children and youth make up nearly one-third of the world population. Governments are urged to combat abuse of the rights of youth, especially females in certain cultures, and to ensure that all children have access to education.

Chapter 26

INDIGENOUS PEOPLE: Indigenous people comprise about 4% of the world's population and their numbers are decreasing. Governments and international organizations should protect their rights and patrimony, recognize their traditional knowledge and resource management practices and enroll them in full global partnership.

Chapter 27

NON-GOVERNMENTAL ORGANIZATIONS: Non-governmental organizations (NGOs) form a network in both developed and developing countries and play a vital role in the shaping and implementation of participatory democracy which is integral to the implementation of sustainable development.

Chapter 28

LOCAL AUTHORITIES: Local authorities, such as municipal governments, should consult citizens and community, business and industrial groups on local programs, policies, laws and regulations to achieve Agenda 21's objectives.

Chapter 29

WORKERS and TRADE UNIONS: Workers will be among those most affected by the changes needed to achieve sustainable development. Through elected representatives, workers must be involved in promoting socially responsible economic development.

Chapter 30

BUSINESS and INDUSTRY: Responsible behavior in the private sector is a prerequisite to achieving sustainable development. Entrepreneurship can play a major role in improving the efficiency of resource use, minimizing wastes and protecting human health and environmental quality.

Chapter 31

SCIENCE and TECHNOLOGY: Scientists and technologists (engineers, architects, industrial designers, urban planners, and other professionals) have special responsibilities to search for knowledge and to help protect the biosphere.

Chapter 32

FARMERS: Farmers are directly responsible for one third

of the land surface of the Earth. They require economic and technical assistance that will encourage them to implement self-sufficient, low-input and low-energy agricultural practices. Women, who do much of the world's farming, should have access to tenure and the use of land, to credits and technologies.

PART FOUR- WHERE DO WE START

Chapter 33

FINANCIAL RESOURCES: Developing nations need free trade and access to markets in order to achieve sustainable economic growth. Special attention should be given to nations whose economies are in transition.

Chapter 34

Transfer of TECHNOLOGY: Scientific knowledge can help prevent shortages of energy, water and non-renewable resources. Developing countries should access environmentally-sound technology and know-how through a collaborative international network of laboratories.

Chapter 35

SCIENCE for Sustainable Development: In the face of threats of irreversible environmental damage, improved knowledge of the Earth's systems is crucial as well as the integration of the natural, social and engineering sciences.

Chapter 36

EDUCATION and PUBLIC AWARENESS: Education gives people the environmental and ethical awareness, values and attitudes, skills and behaviour needed for sustainable development. Because sustainable development must ultimately involve everyone, access to education must be increased for all children and adult illiteracy must be reduced.

Chapter 37

CREATING CAPACITY FOR SUSTAINABLE DEVELOPMENT: All countries share the need to strengthen national capabilities. Developing countries especially need to build their own capacity to implement Agenda 21 in cooperation with UN organizations, developed countries and with each other.

Chapter 38

INTERNATIONAL INSTITUTIONAL ARRANGEMENTS: A large responsibility for following-up with Agenda 21 rests with the United Nations organizations. It is recommended that the UN create a high-level Commission on Sustainable Development which would draw on expertise of UN organizations, international financial organizations and NGOs, industry, business and scientific groups.

Chapter 39

INTERNATIONAL LAW AND MECHANISMS: It is essential that all countries and all sectors within countries, participate in the negotiation of international agreements that create effective international standards for environmental protection.

Chapter 40

SHARING INFORMATION AND DATA FOR DECISION-MAKING: In order to base decisions on sound information, the availability, quality and accessibility of data needs to be improved between developed and developing countries.

Hague Declaration on the Environment, 1989

The right to live is the right from which all other rights stem. Guaranteeing this right is the paramount duty of those in charge of all States throughout the world.

Today, the very conditions of life on our planet are threatened by the severe attacks to which the earth's atmosphere is subjected.

Authoritative scientific studies have shown the existence and scope of considerable dangers linked in particular to the warming of the atmosphere and to the deterioration of the ozone layer. The latter has already led to action, under the 1985 Vienna Convention for the Protection of the Ozone Layer and the 1987 Montreal Protocol, while the former is being addressed by the Intergovernmental Panel on Climatic Change established by UNEP and WMO, which has just begun its work. In addition the UN General Assembly adopted Resolution 43/53 on the Protection of the Global Climate in 1988, recognizing climate change as a common concern of mankind.

According to present scientific knowledge, the consequences of these phenomena may well jeopardize ecological systems as well as the most vital interests of mankind at large.

Because the problem is planet-wide in scope, solutions can only be devised on a global level. Because of the nature of the dangers involved, remedies to be sought involve not only the fundamental duty to preserve the ecosystem, but also the right to live in dignity in a viable global environment, and the consequent duty of the community of nations vis-a-vis present and future generations to do all that can be done to preserve the quality of the atmosphere.

Therefore we consider that, faced with a problem the solution to which has three salient features, namely that it is vital, urgent and global, we are in a situation that calls not only for implementation of existing principles but also for a new approach, through the development of new principles of international law including new and more effective decision-making and enforcement mechanisms.

What is needed here are regulatory, supportive and adjustment measures that take into account the participation and potential contribution of countries which have reached different levels of development. Most of the emissions that affect the atmosphere at present originate in the industrialized nations. And it is in these same nations that the room for change is greatest, and these nations are also those which have the greatest resources to deal with this problem effectively.

The international community and especially the industrialized nations have special obligations to assist developing countries which will be very negatively affected by changes in the atmosphere although the responsibility of many of them for the process may only be marginal today.

Financial institutions and development agencies, be they international or domestic, must coordinate their activities in order to promote sustainable development.

Without prejudice to the international obligations of each State, the signatories acknowledge and will promote the following principles:

(a) The principle of developing, within the framework of the United Nations, new institutional authority, either by strengthening existing institutions or by creating a new institution, which, in the context of the preservation of the earth's atmosphere, shall be responsible for combating any further global warming of the atmosphere and shall involve such decision-making procedures as may be effective even if, on occasion, unanimous agreement has not been achieved;

(b) The principle that this institutional authority undertake or commission the necessary studies, be granted appropriate information upon request, ensure the circulation and exchange of scientific and technological information - including facilitation of access to the technology needed - develop instruments and define standards to enhance or guarantee the protection of the atmosphere and monitor compliance herewith;

(c) The principle of appropriate measures to promote the effective implementation of and compliance with the decisions of the new institutional authority, decisions which will be subject to control by the International Court of Justice;

(d) The principle that countries to which decisions taken to protect the atmosphere shall provoke to be an abnormal or special burden, in view, inter alia, of the level of their development and actual responsibility for the deterioration of the atmosphere, shall receive fair and equitable assistance to compensate them for bearing such burden. To this end mechanisms will have to be developed;

(e) The negotiation of the necessary legal instruments to provide an effective and coherent foundation, institutionally and financially, for the aforementioned principles.

The Heads of State and Government or their representatives, who have expressed their endorsement of this Declaration by placing their signatures under it, stress their resolve to promote the principles thus defined by:

- furthering the development of their initiative within the United Nations and in close coordination and collaboration with existing agencies set up under the auspices of the United Nations;

- inviting all States of the world and the international organizations competent in this field to join in developing, taking into account studies by the IPCC, the framework conventions and other legal instruments necessary to establish institutional authority and to implement the other principles stated above to protect the atmosphere and to counter climate change, particularly global warming;
- urging all States of the world and the international organizations competent in this field to sign and ratify conventions relating to the protection of nature and the environment;
- calling upon all States of the world to endorse present declaration.

KYOTO PROTOCOL TO THE UNITED NATIONS FRAMEWORK CONVENTION ON CLIMATE CHANGE, 1997

The Parties to this Protocol, Being Parties to the United Nations Framework Convention on Climate Change, hereinafter referred to as the Convention, In pursuit of the ultimate objective of the Convention as stated in its Article 2, Recalling the provisions of the Convention, Being guided by Article 3 of the Convention, Pursuant to the Berlin Mandate adopted by decision 1/CP.1 of the Conference of the Parties to the Convention at its first session, Have agreed as follows:

ARTICLE 1

For the purposes of this Protocol, the definitions contained in Article 1 of the Convention shall apply. In addition:

1. Conference of the Parties means the Conference of the Parties to the Convention. UKY.97- FCCC/CP/1997/L.7/ Add.1
2. Conventions means the United Nations Framework Convention on Climate Change, adopted in New York on 9 May 1992.
3. Intergovernmental Panel on Climate Changes means the Intergovernmental Panel on Climate Change established in 1988 jointly by the World Meteorological Organization and the United Nations Environment Programme.
4. Montreal Protocol means the Montreal Protocol on Substances that Deplete the Ozone Layer, adopted in

Montreal on 16 September 1987 and as subsequently adjusted and amended.

5. Parties present and voting means Parties present and casting an affirmative or negative vote.

6. Party means, unless the context otherwise indicates, a Party to this Protocol.

7. Party included in Annex I means a Party included in Annex I to the Convention, as may be amended, or a Party which has made a notification under Article 4, paragraph 2(g), of the Convention.

ARTICLE 2

Each Party included in Annex I in achieving its quantified emission limitation and reduction commitments under Article 3, in order to promote sustainable development, shall:

(a) Implement and/or further elaborate policies and measures in accordance with its national circumstances, such as:

(i) Enhancement of energy efficiency in relevant sectors of the national economy;

(ii) Protection and enhancement of sinks and reservoirs of greenhouse gases not controlled by the Montreal Protocol, taking into account its commitments under relevant international environmental agreements; promotion of sustainable forest management practices, afforestation and reforestation;

(iii) Promotion of sustainable forms of agriculture in light of climate change considerations;

(iv) Promotion, research, development and increased use of new and renewable forms of energy, of carbon dioxide sequestration technologies and of advanced and innovative environmentally sound technologies; FCCC/CP/1997/L.7/Add.1;

(v) Progressive reduction or phasing out of market imperfections, fiscal incentives, tax and duty exemptions and subsidies in all greenhouse gas emitting sectors that run counter to the objective of the Convention and apply market instruments;

(vi) Encouragement of appropriate reforms in relevant sectors aimed at promoting policies and measures which limit or reduce emissions of greenhouse gases not controlled by the Montreal Protocol;

(vii) Measures to limit and/or reduce emissions of greenhouse gases not control led by the Montreal Protocol in the transport sector;

(viii) Limitation and/or reduction of methane through recovery and use in waste management, as well as in the production, transport and distribution of energy;

(b) Cooperate with other such Parties to enhance the individual and combined effectiveness of their policies and measures adopted under this Article, pursuant to Article 4, paragraph 2(e)(i), of the Convention. To this end, these Parties shall take steps to share their experience and exchange information on such policies and measures, including developing ways of improving their comparability, transparency and effectiveness. The Conference of the Parties serving as the meeting of the Parties to this Protocol shall, at its first session or as soon as practicable thereafter, consider ways to facilitate such cooperation, taking into account all relevant information. The Parties included in Annex I shall pursue limitation or reduction of emissions of greenhouse gases not controlled by the Montreal Protocol from aviation and marine bunker fuels, working through the International Civil Aviation Organization and the International Maritime Organization, respectively.

The Parties included in Annex I shall strive to implement policies and measures under this Article in such a way as to minimize adverse effects, including the adverse effects of climate change, effects on international trade, and social, environmental and economic impacts on other Parties, especially developing country Parties and in particular those identified in Article 4, paragraphs 8 and 9 of the Convention, taking into account Article 3 of the Convention. The Conference of the Parties serving as the meeting of the Parties to this Protocol may take further action, as appropriate, to promote the implementation of the provisions of this paragraph. The Conference of the Parties serving as the meeting of the Parties to this Protocol, if it decides that it would be beneficial to coordinate any of the policies and measures in paragraph 1(a) above, taking into account different national circumstances and potential effects, shall consider ways and means to elaborate the coordination of such policies and measures.

ARTICLE 3

1. The Parties included in Annex I shall, individually or jointly, ensure that their aggregate anthropogenic carbon dioxide equivalent emissions of the greenhouse gases listed in Annex A do not exceed their assigned amounts, calculated pursuant to their quantified emission limitation and reduction commitments inscribed in Annex B and in accordance with the provisions of this Article, with a view to reducing their overall emissions of such gases by at least 5 per cent below 1990 levels in the commitment period 2008 to 2012.

2. Each Party included in Annex I shall, by 2005, have made demonstrable progress in achieving its commitments under this Protocol.

3. The net changes in greenhouse gas emissions from sources and removals by sinks resulting from direct human-induced land use change and forestry activities, limited to afforestation, reforestation, and deforestation since 1990, measured as verifiable changes in stocks in each commitment period shall be used to meet the commitments in this Article of each Party included in Annex I. The greenhouse gas emissions from sources and removals by sinks associated with those activities shall be reported in a

transparent and verifiable manner and reviewed in accordance with Articles 7 and 8.

4. Prior to the first session of the Conference of the Parties serving as the meeting of the Parties to this Protocol, each Party included in Annex I shall provide for consideration by the Subsidiary Body for Scientific and Technological Advice data to establish its level of carbon stocks in 1990 and to enable an estimate to be made of its changes in carbon stocks in subsequent years. The Conference of the Parties serving as the meeting of the Parties to this Protocol shall, at its first session or as soon as practicable thereafter, decide upon modalities, rules and guidelines as to how and which additional human-induced activities related to changes in greenhouse gas emissions and removals in the agricultural soil and land use change and forestry categories, shall be added to, or subtracted from, the assigned amount for Parties included in Annex I, taking into account uncertainties, transparency in reporting, verifiability, the methodological work of the Intergovernmental Panel on Climate Change, the advice provided by the Subsidiary Body for Scientific and Technological Advice in accordance with Article 5 and the decisions of the Conference of the Parties. Such a decision shall apply in the second and subsequent commitment periods. A Party may choose to apply such a decision on these additional human-induced activities for its first commitment period, provided that these activities have taken place since 1990.

5. The Parties included in Annex I undergoing the process of transition to a market economy whose base year or period was established pursuant to decision 9/CP.2 of the Conference of the Parties at its second session, shall use that base year or period for the implementation of their commitments under this Article. Any other Party included in Annex I undergoing the process of transition to a market

economy which has not yet submitted its first national communication under Article 12 of the Convention may also notify the

Conference of the Parties serving as the meeting of the Parties to this Protocol that it intends to use a historical base year or period other than 1990 for the implementation of its commitments under this Article. The Conference of the Parties serving as the meeting of the Parties to this Protocol shall decide on the acceptance of such notification.

6. Taking into account Article 4, paragraph 6, of the Convention, in the implementation of their commitments under this Protocol other than those in this Article, a certain degree of flexibility shall be allowed by the Conference of the Parties serving as the meeting of the Parties to this Protocol to the Parties included in Annex I undergoing the process of transition to a market economy.

7. In the first quantified emission limitation and reduction commitment period, from 2008 to 2012, the assigned amount for each Party included in Annex I shall be equal to the percentage inscribed for it in Annex B of its aggregate anthropogenic carbon dioxide equivalent emissions of the greenhouse gases listed in Annex A in 1990, or the base year or period determined in accordance with paragraph 5 above, multiplied by five. Those Parties included in Annex I for whom land use change and forestry constituted a net source of greenhouse gas emissions in 1990 shall include in their 1990 emissions base year or period the aggregate anthropogenic carbon dioxide equivalent emissions minus removals in 1990 from land use change for the purposes of calculating their assigned amount.

8. Any Party included in Annex I may use 1995 as its base year for hydro fluorocarbons, per fluorocarbons and sulphur hexafluoride, for the purposes of the calculation referred to in paragraph 7 above.

9. Commitments for subsequent periods for Parties included in Annex I shall be established in amendments to Annex B to this Protocol, which shall be adopted in accordance with the provisions of 20, paragraph 7. The Conference of the Parties serving as the meeting of the Parties to this Protocol shall initiate the consideration of such commitments at least seven years before the end of the first commitment period mentioned in paragraph 7 above.
10. Any emission reduction units, or any part of an assigned amount, which a Party acquires from another Party in accordance with the provisions of Article 6 and of Article 16 b is shall be added to the assigned amount for that Party.
11. Any emission reduction units, or any part of an assigned amount, which a Party transfers to another Party in accordance with the provisions of Article 6 and of Article 16 b is shall be subtracted from the assigned amount for that Party.
12. Any certified emission reductions which a Party acquires from another Party in accordance with the provisions of Article 12 shall be added to the assigned amount for that Party.
13. If the emissions of a Party included in Annex I during a commitment period are less than its assigned amount under this Article, this difference shall, on request of that Party, be added to the assigned amount for that Party for subsequent commitment periods.
14. Each Party included in Annex I shall strive to implement the commitments mentioned in paragraph 1 above in such a way as to minimize adverse social, environmental and economic impacts on developing country Parties, particularly those identified in Article 4, paragraphs 8 and 9, of the Convention. In line with relevant decisions of the Conference of the Parties on the implementation of those paragraphs, the Conference of the Parties serving as the

meeting of the Parties to this Protocol shall, at its first session, consider what actions are necessary to minimize the adverse effects of climate change and/or the impacts of response measures on Parties referred to in those paragraphs. Among the issues to be considered shall be the establishment of funding, insurance and transfer of technology.

ARTICLE 4

1. Any Parties included in Annex I that have agreed to jointly fulfil their commitments under Article 3 shall be deemed to have met those commitments provided that their total combined aggregate anthropogenic carbon dioxide equivalent emissions of the greenhouse gases listed in Annex A do not exceed their assigned amounts calculated pursuant to their quantified emission limitation and reduction commitments inscribed in Annex B and in accordance with the provisions of Article 3. The respective emission level allocated to each of the Parties to the agreement shall be set out in that agreement.

2. The Parties to any such agreement shall notify the secretariat of the terms of the agreement on the date of deposit of their instruments of ratification, acceptance, approval or accession. The secretariat shall in turn inform the Parties and signatories to the Convention of the terms of the agreement.

3. The agreement shall remain in operation for the duration of the commitment period specified in Article 3, paragraph 7.

4. If Parties acting jointly do so in the framework of, and together with, a regional economic integration organization, any alteration in the composition of the organization after adoption of this Protocol shall not affect existing commitments under this Protocol. Any alteration in the composition of the organization shall only apply for the purposes of those commitments under Article 3 that are adopted subsequent to that revision.

5. In the event of failure by the Parties to such an agreement to achieve their total combined level of emission reductions, each Party to such an agreement shall be responsible for its own level of emissions set out in the agreement.
6. If Parties acting jointly do so in the framework of, and together with, a regional economic integration organization which is itself a Party to this Protocol, each member State of that regional economic integration organization individually, and together with the regional economic integration organization acting in accordance with Article 23, shall, in the event of failure to achieve the total combined level of emission reductions, be responsible for its level of emissions as notified in accordance with this Article.

ARTICLE 5

1. Each Party included in Annex I shall have in place, no later than one year prior to the start of the first commitment period, a national system for the estimation of anthropogenic emissions by sources and removals by sinks of all greenhouse gases not controlled by the Montreal Protocol. Guidelines for such national systems, which shall incorporate the methodologies specified in paragraph 2 below, shall be decided upon by the Conference of the Parties serving as the meeting of the Parties to this Protocol at its first session.
2. Methodologies for estimating anthropogenic emissions by sources and removals by sinks of all greenhouse gases not controlled by the Montreal Protocol shall be those accepted by the Intergovernmental Panel on Climate Change and agreed upon by the Conference of the Parties at its third session. Where such methodologies are not used, appropriate adjustments shall be applied according to methodologies agreed upon by the Conference of the Parties serving as the meeting of the Parties to this Protocol

at its first session. Based on the work of, inter alia, the Intergovernmental Panel on Climate Change and advice provided by the Subsidiary Body for Scientific and Technological Advice, the Conference of the Parties serving as the meeting of the Parties to this Protocol shall regularly review and, as appropriate, revise such methodologies and adjustments, taking fully into account any relevant decisions by the Conference of the Parties. Any revision to methodologies or adjustments shall be used only for the purposes of ascertaining compliance with commitments under Article 3 in respect of any commitment period adopted subsequent to that revision.

3. The global warming potentials used to calculate the carbon dioxide equivalence of anthropogenic emissions by sources and removals by sinks of greenhouse gases not controlled by the Montreal Protocol listed in Annex A shall be those accepted by the Intergovernmental Panel on Climate Change and agreed upon by the Conference of the Parties at its third session. Based on the work of, inter alia, the Intergovernmental Panel on Climate Change and advice provided by the Subsidiary Body for Scientific and Technological Advice, the Conference of the Parties serving as the meeting of the Parties to this Protocol shall regularly review and, as appropriate, revise the global warming potential of each such greenhouse gas, taking fully into account any relevant decisions by the Conference of the Parties. Any revision to a global warming potential shall apply only to those commitments under Article 3 in respect of any commitment period adopted subsequent to that revision.

ARTICLE 6

1. For the purpose of meeting its commitments under Article 3, any Party included in Annex I may transfer to, or acquire from, any other such Party emission reduction units resulting from projects aimed at reducing anthropogenic

emissions by sources or enhancing anthropogenic removals by sinks of greenhouse gases in any sector of the economy, provided that:

(a) Any such project has the approval of the Parties involved;

(b) Any such project provides a reduction in emissions by sources, or an enhancement of removals by sinks, that is additional to any that would otherwise occur;

(c) It does not acquire any emission reduction units if it is not in compliance with its obligations under Articles 5 and 7;

(d) The acquisition of emission reduction units shall be supplemental to domestic actions for the purposes of meeting commitments under Article 3.

2. The Conference of the Parties serving as the meeting of the Parties to this Protocol may, at its first session or as soon as practicable thereafter, further elaborate guidelines for the implementation of this Article, including for verification and reporting.

3. A Party included in Annex I may authorize legal entities to participate, under its responsibility, in actions leading to the generation, transfer or acquisition under this Article of emission reduction units.

4. If a question of implementation by a Party included in Annex I of the requirements referred to in this paragraph is identified in accordance with the relevant provisions of Article 8, transfers and acquisitions of emission reduction units may continue to be made after the question has been identified, provided that any such units may not be used by a Party to meet its commitments under Article 3 until any issue of compliance is resolved.

ARTICLE 7

1. Each Party included in Annex I shall incorporate in its

annual inventory of anthropogenic emissions by sources and removals by sinks of greenhouse gases not controlled by the Montreal Protocol, submitted in accordance with the relevant decisions of the Conference of the Parties, the necessary supplementary information for the purposes of ensuring compliance with Article 3, to be determined in accordance with paragraph 4 below.

2. Each Party included in Annex I shall incorporate in its national communication, submitted under Article 12 of the Convention, the supplementary information necessary to demonstrate compliance with its commitments under this Protocol, to be determined in accordance with paragraph 4 below.

3. Each Party included in Annex I shall submit the information required under paragraph 1 above annually, beginning with the first inventory due under the Convention for the first year of the commitment period after this Protocol has entered into force for it. Each such Party shall submit the information required under paragraph 2 above as part of the first national communication due under the Convention after this Protocol has entered into force for it and after the adoption of guidelines as provided for in paragraph 4 below. The frequency of subsequent submission of information required under this Article shall be determined by the Conference of the Parties serving as the meeting of the Parties to this Protocol, taking into account any timetable for the submission of national communications decided upon by the Conference of the Parties.

4. The Conference of the Parties serving as the meeting of the Parties to this Protocol shall adopt at its first session, and review periodically thereafter, guidelines for the preparation of the information required under this Article, taking into account guidelines for the preparation of national communications by Parties included in Annex I

adopted by the Conference of the Parties. The Conference of the Parties serving as the meeting of the Parties to this Protocol shall also, prior to the first commitment period, decide upon modalities for the accounting of assigned amounts.

ARTICLE 8

1. The information submitted under Article 7 by each Party included in Annex I shall be reviewed by expert review teams pursuant to the relevant decisions of the Conference of the Parties and in accordance with guidelines adopted for this purpose by the Conference of the Parties serving as the meeting of the Parties to this Protocol under paragraph 4 below. The information submitted under Article 7, paragraph 1, by each Party included in Annex I shall be reviewed as part of the annual compilation and accounting of emissions inventories and assigned amounts. Additionally, the information submitted under Article 7, paragraph 2, by each Party included in Annex I shall be reviewed as part of the review of communications.
2. Expert review teams shall be coordinated by the secretariat and shall be composed of experts selected from those nominated by Parties to the Convention and, as appropriate, by intergovernmental organizations, in accordance with guidance provided for this purpose by the Conference of the Parties.
3. The review process shall provide a thorough and comprehensive technical assessment of all aspects of the implementation by a Party of this Protocol. The expert review teams shall prepare a report to the Conference of the Parties serving as the meeting of the Parties to this Protocol, assessing the implementation of the commitments of the Party and identifying any potential problems in, and factors influencing, the fulfilment of commitments. Such reports shall be circulated by the secretariat to all Parties

to the Convention. The secretariat shall list those questions of implementation indicated in such reports for further consideration by the Conference of the Parties serving as the meeting of the Parties to this Protocol.

4. The Conference of the Parties serving as the meeting of the Parties to this Protocol shall adopt at its first session, and review periodically thereafter, guidelines for the review of implementation by expert review teams taking into account the relevant decisions of the Conference of the Parties.

5. The Conference of the Parties serving as the meeting of the Parties to this Protocol shall, with the assistance of the Subsidiary Body for Implementation and, as appropriate, the Subsidiary Body for Scientific and Technological Advice, consider:

   (a) The information submitted by the Parties under Article 7 and the reports of the expert reviews thereon conducted under this Article; and

   (b) Those questions of implementation listed by the secretariat under paragraph 3 above, as well as any questions raised by Parties .

6. Pursuant to its consideration of the information referred to in paragraph 5 above, the Conference of the Parties serving as the meeting of the Parties to this Protocol shall take decisions on any matter required for the implementation of this Protocol.

ARTICLE 9

1. The Conference of the Parties serving as the meeting of the Parties to this Protocol shall periodically review this Protocol in the light of the best available scientific information and assessments on climate change and its impacts, as well as relevant technical, social and economic information. Such reviews shall be coordinated with pertinent reviews under the Convention, in particular those

required by Article 4, paragraph 2(d), and Article 7, paragraph 2(a), of the Convention. Based on these reviews, the Conference of the Parties serving as the meeting of the Parties to this Protocol shall take appropriate action.

2. The first review shall take place at the second session of the Conference of the Parties serving as the meeting of the Parties to this Protocol. Further reviews shall take place at regular intervals and in a timely manner.

ARTICLE 10

1. All Parties, taking into account their common but differentiated responsibilities and their specific national and regional development priorities, objectives and circumstances, without introducing any new commitments for Parties not included in Annex I, but reaffirming existing commitments in Article 4, paragraph 1, of the Convention, and continuing to advance the implementation of these commitments in order to achieve sustainable development; taking into account Article 4, paragraphs 3, 5 and 7, of the Convention, shall:

(a) Formulate, where relevant and to the extent possible, cost-effective national, and where appropriate regional programmes to improve the quality of local emission factors, activity data and/or models which reflect the socio-economic conditions of each Party for the preparation and periodic updating of national inventories of anthropogenic emissions by sources and removals by sinks of all greenhouse gases not controlled by the Montreal Protocol, using comparable methodologies to be agreed upon by the Conference of the Parties, and consistent with the guidelines for national communications adopted by the Conference of the Parties;

(b) Formulate, implement, publish and regularly update national and, where appropriate, regional programmes containing measures to mitigate climate change and measures to facilitate adequate adaptation to climate change:

(i) Such programmes would, inter alia, concern the energy, transport and industry sectors as well as agriculture, forestry and waste management. Furthermore, adaptation technologies and methods for improving spatial planning would improve adaptation to climate change; and

(ii) Parties included in Annex I shall submit information on action under this Protocol, including national programmes, according to the guidelines laid down in Article 8; and other Parties shall seek to include in their national communications, as appropriate, information on programmes which contain measures that the Party believes contribute to addressing climate change and its adverse impacts, including the abatement of increase in greenhouse gas emissions, and enhancement of and removals by sinks, capacity building and adaptation measures.

(c) Cooperate in the promotion of effective modalities for the development, application and diffusion of, and take all practicable steps to promote, facilitate and finance, as appropriate, the transfer of, or access to, environmentally sound technologies, know-how, practices and processes pertinent to climate change, in particular to developing countries, including the formulation of policies and programmes for the effective transfer of environmentally sound technologies that are publicly owned or in the public domain and the creation of an enabling environment for the private sector, to promote and enhance access to, and transfer of, environmentally sound technologies;

(d) Cooperate in scientific and technical research and promote the maintenance and the development of systematic observation systems and development of data archives to reduce uncertainties related to the climate system, the adverse impacts of climate change and the economic and social consequences of various response strategies, and promote the development and strengthening of endogenous capacities and capabilities to participate in international and intergovernmental efforts, programmes and networks on research and systematic observation, taking into account Article 5 of the Convention;

(e) Cooperate in and promote at the international level, and, where appropriate, using existing bodies, the development and implementation of education and training programmes, including the strengthening of national capacity building, in particular human and institutional capacities and the exchange or secondment of personnel to train experts in this field, in particular for developing countries, and facilitate at the national level public awareness and public access to information on climate change. Suitable modalities should be developed to implement these activities through the relevant bodies of the Convention taking into account Article 6 of the Convention;

(f) Include in their national communications information on programmes and activities undertaken pursuant to this Article in accordance with relevant decisions of the Conference of the Parties; and

(g) Give full consideration, in implementing the commitments in this Article, to Article 4, paragraph 8, of the Convention.

ARTICLE 11

1. In the implementation of Article 10, Parties shall take into account the provisions of Article 4, paragraphs 4, 5, 7, 8 and 9 of the Convention.

2. In the context of the implementation of Article 4, paragraph 1, of the Convention, in accordance with the provisions of Article 4, paragraph 3, and Article 11 of the Convention, and through the operating entity or entities of the financial

mechanism of the Convention, the developed country Parties and other developed Parties included in Annex II to the Convention shall:

(a) Provide new and additional financial resources to meet the agreed full costs incurred by developing country Parties in advancing the implementation of existing commitments under Article 4, paragraph 1(a), of the Convention that are covered in Article 10, subparagraph (a); and

(b) Also provide such financial resources, including for the transfer of technology, needed by the developing country Parties to meet the agreed full incremental costs of advancing the implementation of existing commitments in Article 4, paragraph 1, of the Convention that are covered by Article 10 and that are agreed between a developing country Party and the international entity or entities referred to in Article 11 of the Convention, in accordance with that Article.

The implementation of these existing commitments shall take into account the need for adequacy and predictability in the flow of funds and the importance of appropriate burden sharing among developed country Parties. The guidance to the financial mechanism of the Convention in relevant decisions of the Conference of the Parties, including those agreed before the adoption of this Protocol, shall apply mutatis mutandis to the provisions of this paragraph. 3. The developed country Parties and other developed Parties in Annex II to the Convention may also provide, and developing country Parties avail themselves of, financial resources for the implementation of Article 10, through bilateral, regional and other multilateral channels.

ARTICLE 12

1. A clean development mechanism is hereby defined.
2. The purpose of the clean development mechanism shall be to assist Parties not included in Annex I in achieving

sustainable development and in contributing to the ultimate objective of the Convention, and to assist Parties included in Annex I in achieving compliance with their quantified emission limitation and reduction commitments under Article 3.

3. Under the clean development mechanism:

   (a) Parties not included in Annex I will benefit from project activities resulting in certified emission reductions; and

   (b) Parties included in Annex I may use the certified emission reductions accruing from such project activities to contribute to compliance with part of their quantified emission limitation and reduction commitments under Article 3, as determined by the Conference of the Parties serving as the meeting of the Parties to this Protocol.

4. The clean development mechanism shall be subject to the authority and guidance of the Conference of the Parties serving as the meeting of the Parties to this Protocol and be supervised by an executive board of the clean development mechanism.

5. Emission reductions resulting from each project activity shall be certified by operational entities to be designated by the Conference of the Parties serving as the meeting of the Parties to this Protocol, on the basis of:

   (a) Voluntary participation approved by each Party involved;

   (b) Real, measurable, and long-term benefits related to the mitigation of climate change; and FCCC/CP/1997/L.7/Add.1 English Page 14 (c) Reductions in emissions that are additional to any that would occur in the absence of the certified project activity.

6. The clean development mechanism shall assist in arranging funding of certified project activities as necessary.

7. The Conference of the Parties serving as the meeting of the Parties to this Protocol shall, at its first session, elaborate modalities and procedures with the objective of ensuring transparency, efficiency and accountability through independent auditing and verification of project activities.
8. The Conference of the Parties serving as the meeting of the Parties to this Protocol shall ensure that a share of the proceeds from certified project activities is used to cover administrative expenses as well as to assist developing country Parties that are particularly vulnerable to the adverse effects of climate change to meet the costs of adaptation.
9. Participation under the clean development mechanism, including in activities mentioned in paragraph 3(a) above and acquisition of certified emission reductions, may involve private and/or public entities, and is to be subject to whatever guidance may be provided by the executive board of the clean development mechanism.
10. Certified emission reductions obtained during the period from the year 2000 up to the beginning of the first commitment period can be used to assist in achieving compliance in the first commitment period.

ARTICLE 13

1. The Conference of the Parties. the supreme body of the Convention, shall serve as the meeting of the Parties to this Protocol.
2. Parties to the Convention that are not Parties to this Protocol may participate as observers in the proceedings of any session of the Conference of the Parties serving as the meeting of the Parties to this Protocol. When the Conference of the Parties serves as the meeting of the Parties to this Protocol, decisions under this Protocol shall be taken only by those that are Parties to it.

3. When the Conference of the Parties serves as the meeting of the Parties to this Protocol, any member of the Bureau of the Conference of the Parties representing a Party to the Convention but, at that time, not a Party to this Protocol, shall be substituted by an additional member to be elected by and from amongst the Parties to this Protocol.

4. The Conference of the Parties serving as the meeting of the Parties to this Protocol shall keep under regular review the implementation of this Protocol and shall make, within its mandate, the decisions necessary to promote its effective implementation. It shall perform the functions assigned to it by this Protocol and shall:

   (a) Assess, on the basis of all information made available to it in accordance with the provisions of this Protocol, the implementation of this Protocol by the Parties, the overall effects of the measures taken pursuant to this Protocol, in particular environmental, economic and social effects as well as their cumulative impacts and the extent to which progress towards the objective of the Convention is being achieved;

   (b) Periodically examine the obligations of the Parties under this Protocol, giving due consideration to any reviews required by Article 4, paragraph 2(d), and Article 7, paragraph 2, of the Convention, in the light of the objective of the Convention, the experience gained in its implementation and the evolution of scientific and technological knowledge, and in this respect consider and adopt regular reports on the implementation of this Protocol;

   (c) Promote and facilitate the exchange of information on measures adopted by the Parties to address climate change and its effects, taking into account the differing circumstances, responsibilities and capabilities of the Parties and their respective commitments under this Protocol;

(d) Facilitate, at the request of two or more Parties, the coordination of measures adopted by them to address climate change and its effects, taking into account the differing circumstances, responsibilities and capabilities of the Parties and their respective commitments under this Protocol;

(e) Promote and guide, in accordance with the objective of the Convention of this Protocol, and taking fully into account the relevant decisions by the Conference of the Parties, the development and periodic refinement of comparable methodologies for the effective implementation of this Protocol, to be agreed on by the Conference of the Parties serving as the meeting of the Parties to this Protocol;

(f) Make recommendations on any matters necessary for the implementation of this Protocol;

(g) Seek to mobilize additional financial resources in accordance with Article 11, paragraph 2;

(h) Establish such subsidiary bodies as are deemed necessary for the implementation of this Protocol;

(i) Seek and utilize, where appropriate, the services and cooperation of, and information provided by, competent international organizations and intergovernmental and non-governmental bodies; and

(j) Exercise such other functions as may be required for the implementation of this Protocol, and consider any assignment resulting from a decision by the Conference of the Parties.

5. The rules of procedure of the Conference of the Parties and financial procedures of the Convention shall be applied mutatis mutandis under this Protocol, except as maybe otherwise decided by consensus by the Conference of the Parties serving as the meeting of the Parties to this Protocol.

6. The first session of the Conference of the Parties serving

as the meeting of the Parties to this Protocol shall be convened by the secretariat in conjunction with the first session of the Conference of the Parties that is scheduled after the date of the entry into force of this Protocol. Subsequent ordinary sessions of the Conference of the Parties serving as the meeting of the Parties to this Protocol shall be held every year and in conjunction with ordinary sessions of the Conference of the Parties unless otherwise decided by the Conference of the Parties serving as the meeting of the Parties to this Protocol.

7. Extraordinary sessions of the Conference of the Parties serving as the meeting of the Parties to this Protocol shall be held at such other times as may be deemed necessary by the Conference of the Parties serving as the meeting of the Parties to this Protocol, or at the written request of any Party, provided that, within six months of the request being communicated to the Parties by the secretariat, it is supported by at least one third of the Parties.

8. The United Nations, its specialized agencies and the International Atomic Energy Agency, as well as any State member thereof or observers thereto not party to the Convention, maybe represented at sessions of the Conference of the Parties serving as the meeting of the Parties to this Protocol as observers. Any body or agency, whether national or international, governmental or non-governmental, which is qualified in matters covered by this Protocol and which has informed the secretariat of its wish to be represented at a session of the Conference of the Parties serving as the meeting of the Parties to this Protocol as an observer, may be so admitted unless at least one third of the Parties present object. The admission and participation of observers shall be subject to the rules of procedure, as referred to in paragraph 5 above.

ARTICLE 14

1. The secretariat established by Article 8 of the Convention shall serve as the secretariat of this Protocol.
2. Article 8, paragraph 2, of the Convention on the functions of the secretariat, and Article 8, paragraph 3, of the Convention on arrangements made for the functioning of the secretariat, shall apply mutatis mutandis to this Protocol. The secretariat shall, in addition, exercise the functions assigned to it under this Protocol.

ARTICLE 15

1. The Subsidiary Body for Scientific and Technological Advice and the Subsidiary Body for Implementation established by Articles 9 and 10 of the Convention shall serve as, respectively, the Subsidiary Body for Scientific and Technological Advice and the Subsidiary Body for Implementation of this Protocol. The provisions relating to the functioning of these two bodies under the Convention shall apply mutatis mutandis to this Protocol. Sessions of the meetings of the Subsidiary Body for Scientific and Technological Advice and the Subsidiary Body for Implementation of this Protocol shall be held in conjunction with the meetings of, respectively, the Subsidiary Body for Scientific and Technological Advice and the Subsidiary Body for Implementation of the Convention.
2. Parties to the Convention that are not Parties to this Protocol may participate as observers in the proceedings of any session of the subsidiary bodies. When the subsidiary bodies serve as the subsidiary bodies of this Protocol, decisions under this Protocol shall be taken only by the Parties to this Protocol.
3. When the subsidiary bodies established by Articles 9 and 10 of the Convention exercise their functions with regard to matters concerning this Protocol, any member of the

Bureaux of those subsidiary bodies representing a Party to the Convention but, at that time, not a party to this Protocol, shall be substituted by an additional member to be elected by and from amongst the Parties to this Protocol.

ARTICLE 16

The Conference of the Parties serving as the meeting of the Parties to this Protocol shall, as soon as practicable, consider the application to this Protocol of, and modify as appropriate, the multilateral consultative process referred to in Article 13 of the Convention, in the light of any relevant decisions that may be taken by the Conference of the Parties. Any multilateral consultative process that may be applied to this Protocol shall operate without prejudice to the procedures and mechanisms established in accordance with Article 17.

ARTICLE 16 (B)

The Conference of the Parties shall define the relevant principles, modalities, rules and guidelines, in particular for verification, reporting and accountability for emissions trading. The Parties included in Annex B may participate in emissions trading for the purposes of fulfilling their commitments under Article 3 of this Protocol. Any such trading shall be supplemental to domestic actions for the purpose of meeting quantified emission limitation and reduction commitments under that Article.

ARTICLE 17

The Conference of the Parties serving as the meeting of the Parties to this Protocol shall, at its first session, approve appropriate and effective procedures and mechanisms to determine and to address cases of non-compliance with the provisions of this Protocol, including through the development of an indicative list of consequences, taking into account the cause, type, degree and frequency of non-compliance. Any procedures and mechanisms under this Article entailing binding consequences shall be adopted by means of an amendment to this Protocol.

ARTICLE 18

The provisions of Article 14 of the Convention on settlement of disputes shall apply mutatis mutandis to this Protocol.

ARTICLE 19

1. Any Party may propose amendments to this Protocol.
2. Amendments to this Protocol shall be adopted at an ordinary session of the Conference of the Parties serving as the meeting of the Parties to this Protocol. The text of any proposed amendment to this Protocol shall be communicated to the Parties by the secretariat at least six months before the meeting at which it is proposed for adoption. The secretariat shall also communicate the text of any proposed amendments to the Parties and signatories to the Convention and, for information, to the Depositary.
3. The Parties shall make every effort to reach agreement on any proposed amendment to this Protocol by consensus. If all efforts at consensus have been exhausted, and no agreement reached, the amendment shall as a last resort be adopted by a three-fourths majority vote of the Parties present and voting at the meeting. The adopted amendment shall be communicated by the secretariat to the Depositary, who shall circulate it to all Parties for their acceptance.
4. Instruments of acceptance in respect of an amendment shall be deposited with the Depositary. An amendment adopted in accordance with paragraph 3 above shall enter into force for those Parties having accepted it on the ninetieth day after the date of receipt by the Depositary of an instrument of acceptance by at least three fourths of the Parties to this Protocol.
5. The amendment shall enter into force for any other Party

on the ninetieth day after the date on which that Party deposits with the Depositary its instrument of acceptance of the said amendment.

ARTICLE 20

1. Annexes to this Protocol shall form an integral part thereof and, unless otherwise expressly provided, a reference to this Protocol constitutes at the same time a reference to any annexes thereto. Any annexes adopted after the entry into force of this Protocol shall be restricted to lists, forms and any other material of a descriptive nature that is of a scientific, technical, procedural or administrative character.
2. Any Party may make proposals for an annex to this Protocol and may propose amendments to annexes to this Protocol.
3. Annexes to this Protocol and amendments to annexes to this Protocol shall be adopted at an ordinary session of the Conference of the Parties serving as the meeting of the Parties to this Protocol. The text of any proposed annex or amendment to an annex shall be communicated to the Parties by the secretariat at least six months before the meeting at which it is proposed for adoption. The secretariat shall also communicate the text of any proposed annex or amendment to an annex to the Parties and signatories to the Convention and, for information, to the Depositary.
4. The Parties shall make every effort to reach agreement on any proposed annex or amendment to an annex by consensus. If all efforts at consensus have been exhausted, and no agreement reached, the annex or amendment to an annex shall as a last resort be adopted by a three-fourths majority vote of the Parties present and voting at the meeting. The adopted annex or amendment to an annex shall be communicated by the secretariat to the Depositary, who shall circulate it to all Parties for their acceptance.
5. An annex, other than Annex A or B, that has been adopted

or amended in accordance with paragraphs 3 and 4 above shall enter into force for all Parties to this Protocol six months after the date of the communication by the Depositary to such Parties of the adoption or amendment of the annex, except for those Parties that have notified the Depositary in writing within that period of their non-acceptance of the annex or amendment to the annex. The annex or amendment to an annex shall enter into force for Parties which withdraw their notification of non-acceptance on the ninetieth day after the date on which withdrawal of such notification has been received by the Depositary.

6. If the adoption of an annex or an amendment to an annex involves an amendment to this Protocol, that annex or amendment to an annex shall not enter into force until such time as the amendment to this Protocol enters into force.

7. Amendments to Annexes A and B to this Protocol shall be adopted and enter into force in accordance with the procedure set out in Article 19, provided that any amendments to Annex B shall be adopted only with the written consent of the Party concerned .

ARTICLE 21

1. Each Party shall have one vote, except as provided for in paragraph 2 below.

2. Regional economic integration organizations, in matters within their competence, shall exercise their right to vote with a number of votes equal to the number of their member States which are Parties to this Protocol. Such an organization shall not exercise its right to vote if any of its member States exercises its right, and vice versa.

ARTICLE 22

The Secretary-General of the United Nations shall be the Depositary of this Protocol.

ARTICLE 23

1. This Protocol shall be open for signature and subject to ratification, acceptance or approval by States and regional economic integration organizations which are Parties to the Convention. It shall be open for signature at United Nations Headquarters in New York from 16 March 1998 to 15 March 1999. This Protocol shall be open for accession from the day after the date on which it is closed for signature. Instruments of ratification, acceptance, approval or accession shall be deposited with the Depositary.
2. Any regional economic integration organization which becomes a Party to this Protocol without any of its member States being a Party shall be bound by all the obligations under this Protocol. In the case of such organizations, one or more of whose member States is a Party to this Protocol, the organization and its member States shall decide on their respective responsibilities for the performance of their obligations under this Protocol. In such cases, the organization and the member States shall not be entitled to exercise rights under this Protocol concurrently.
3. In their instruments of ratification, acceptance, approval or accession, regional economic integration organizations shall declare the extent of their competence with respect to the matters governed by this Protocol. These organizations shall also inform the Depositary, who shall in turn inform the Parties, of any substantial modification in the extent of their competence.

ARTICLE 24

1. This Protocol shall enter into force on the ninetieth day after the date on which not less than 55 Parties to the Convention, incorporating Parties included in Annex I which accounted in total for at least 55 per cent of the total carbon dioxide emissions for 1990 of the Parties included in Annex I, have deposited their instruments of ratification, acceptance, approval or accession.

2. For the purposes of this Article, the total carbon dioxide emissions for 1990 of the Parties included in Annex IS means the amount communicated on or before the date of adoption of this Protocol by the Parties included in Annex I in their first national communications submitted in accordance with Article 12 of the Convention.

3. For each State or regional economic integration organization that ratifies, accepts or approves this Protocol or accedes thereto after the conditions set out in paragraph 1 above for the entry into force have been fulfilled, this Protocol shall enter into force on the ninetieth day following the date of deposit of its instrument of ratification, acceptance, approval or accession.

4. For the purposes of this Article, any instrument deposited by a regional economic integration organization shall not be counted as additional to those deposited by States members of the organization.

ARTICLE 25

No reservations may be made to this Protocol.

ARTICLE 26

1. At any time after three years from the date on which this Protocol has entered into force for a Party, that Party may withdraw from this Protocol by giving written notification to the Depositary.

2. Any such withdrawal shall take effect upon expiry of one year from the date of receipt by the Depositary of the notification of withdrawal, or on such later date as may be specified in the notification of withdrawal.

3. Any Party that withdraws from the Convention shall be considered as also having withdrawn from this Protocol.

United Nations International Labour Organisation

ILO Convention 169 - Convention Concerning Indigenous and Tribal Peoples in Independent Countries

The General Conference of the International Labour Organisation,

Having been convened at Geneva by the Governing Body of the International Labour Office, and having met in its 76th Session on 7 June 1989, and

Noting the international standards contained in the Indigenous and Tribal Populations Convention and Recommendation, 1957, and

Recalling the terms of the Universal Declaration of Human Rights, the International Covenant on Economic, Social and Cultural Rights, the International Covenant on Civil and Political Rights, and the many international instruments on the prevention of discrimination, and

Considering that the developments which have taken place in international law since 1957, as well as developments in the situation of indigenous and tribal peoples in all regions of the world, have made it appropriate to adopt new international standards on the subject with a view to removing the assimilationists orientation of the earlier standards, and

Recognising the aspirations of these peoples to exercise control over their own institutions, ways of life and economic development and to maintain and develop their identities, languages and religions, within the framework of the States in which they live, and

Noting that in many parts of the world these peoples are unable to enjoy their fundamental human rights to the same degree as the rest of the population of the States within which they live, and that their laws, values, customs and perspectives have often been eroded, and

Calling attention to the distinctive contributions of indigenous and tribal peoples to the cultural diversity and social and ecological harmony of humankind and to international co-operation and understanding, and

Noting that the following provisions have been framed with the co- operation of the United Nations, the Food and Agriculture Organisation of the United Nations, the United Nations Educational, Scientific and Cultural Organisation and the World Health Organisation, as well as of the Inter-American Indian Institute, at appropriate levels and in their respective fields, and that it is proposed to continue this co-operation in promoting and securing the application of these provisions, and

Having decided upon the adoption of certain proposals with regard to the partial revision of the Indigenous and Tribal Populations Convention, 1957 (No. 107), which is the fourth item on the agenda of the session, and

Having determined that these proposals shall take the form of an international Convention revising the Indigenous and Tribal Populations Convention, 1957;

Adopts this twenty-seventh day of June of the year one thousand nine hundred and eighty-nine the following Convention, which may be cited as the Indigenous and Tribal Peoples Convention, 1989:

PART I - GENERAL POLICY

ARTICLE 1

1. This Convention applies to:

   (a) tribal peoples in independent countries whose social, cultural and economic conditions distinguish them from other sections of the national community and whose status is regulated wholly or partially by their own customs or traditions or by special laws or regulations;

(b) peoples in independent countries who are regarded as indigenous on account of their descent from the populations which inhabited the country, or a geographical region to which the country belongs, at the time of conquest or colonisation or the establishment of present state boundaries and who, irrespective of their legal status, retain some or all of their own social, economic, cultural and political institutions.

2. Self-identification as indigenous or tribal shall be regarded as a fundamental criterion for determining the groups to which the provisions of this Convention apply.

3. The use of the term "peoples" in this Convention shall not be construed as having any implications as regards the rights which may attach to the term under international law.

ARTICLE 2

1. Governments shall have the responsibility for developing, with the participation of the peoples concerned, co-ordinated and systematic action to protect the rights of these peoples and to guarantee respect for their integrity.

2. Such action shall include measures for:

(a) ensuring that members of these peoples benefit on an equal footing from the rights and opportunities which national laws and regulations grant to other members of the population;

(b) promoting the full realisation of the social, economic and cultural rights of these peoples with respect for their social and cultural identity, their customs and traditions and their institutions;

(c) assisting the members of the peoples concerned to eliminate socio-economic gaps that may exist between indigenous and other members of the national community, in a manner compatible with their aspirations and ways of life.

ARTICLE 3

1. Indigenous and tribal peoples shall enjoy the full measure of human rights and fundamental freedoms without hindrance or discrimination. The provisions of the Convention shall be applied without discrimination to male and female members of these peoples.
2. No form of force or coercion shall be used in violation of the human rights and fundamental freedoms of the peoples concerned, including the rights contained in this Convention.

ARTICLE 4

1. Special measures shall be adopted as appropriate for safeguarding the persons, institutions, property, labour, cultures and environment of the peoples concerned.
2. Such special measures shall not be contrary to the freely-expressed wishes of the peoples concerned.
3. Enjoyment of the general rights of citizenship, without discrimination, shall not be prejudiced in any way by such special measures.

ARTICLE 5

In applying the provisions of this Convention:

(a) the social, cultural, religious and spiritual values and practices of these peoples shall be recognised and protected, and due account shall be taken of the nature of the problems which face them both as groups and as individuals;

(b) the integrity of the values, practices and institutions of these peoples shall be respected;

(c) policies aimed at mitigating the difficulties experienced by these peoples in facing new conditions of life and work shall be adopted, with the participation and co-operation of the peoples affected.

ARTICLE 6

1. In applying the provisions of this Convention, governments shall:
   (a) consult the peoples concerned, through appropriate procedures and in particular through their representative institutions, whenever consideration is being given to legislative or administrative measures which may affect them directly;
   (b) establish means by which these peoples can freely participate, to at least the same extent as other sectors of the population, at all levels of decision making in elective institutions and administrative and other bodies responsible for policies and programmes which concern them;
   (c) establish means for the full development of these peoples' own institutions and initiatives, and in appropriate cases provide the resources necessary for this purpose.
2. The consultations carried out in application of this Convention shall be undertaken, in good faith and in a form appropriate to the circumstances, with the objective of achieving agreement or consent to the proposed measures.

ARTICLE 7

1. The peoples concerned shall have the right to decide their own priorities for the process of development as it affects their lives, beliefs, institutions and spiritual well-being and the lands they occupy or otherwise use, and to exercise control, to the extent possible, over their own economic, social and cultural development. In addition, they shall

participate in the formulation, implementation and evaluation of plans and programmes for national and regional development which may affect them directly.

2. The improvement of the conditions of life and work and levels of health and education of the peoples concerned, with their participation and co-operation, shall be a matter of priority in plans for the overall economic development at areas they inhabit. Special projects for development of the areas in question shall also be so designed as to promote such improvement.

3. Governments shall ensure that, whenever appropriate, studies are carried out, in co-operation with the peoples concerned, to assess the social, spiritual, cultural and environmental impact on them of planned development activities. The results of these studies shall be considered as fundamental criteria for the implementation of these activities.

4. Governments shall take measures, in co-operation with the peoples concerned, to protect and preserve the environment of the territories they inhabit.

ARTICLE 8

1. In applying national laws and regulations to the peoples concerned, due regard shall be had to their customs or customary laws.

2. These peoples shall have the right to retain their own customs and institutions, where these are not incompatible with fundamental rights defined by the national legal system and with internationally recognised human rights. Procedures shall be established, whenever necessary, to resolve conflicts which may arise in the application of this principle.

3. The application of paragraphs 1 and 2 of this Article shall not prevent members of these peoples from exercising the rights granted to all citizens and from assuming the corresponding duties.

ARTICLE 9

1. To the extent compatible with the national legal system and internationally recognised human rights, the methods customarily practised by the peoples concerned for dealing with offences committed by their members shall be respected.
2. The customs of these peoples in regard to penal matters shall be taken into consideration by the authorities and courts dealing with such cases.

ARTICLE 10

1. In imposing penalties laid down by general law on members of these peoples account shall be taken of their economic, social and cultural characteristics.
2. Preference shall be given to methods of punishment other than confinement in prison.

ARTICLE 11

The exaction from members of the peoples concerned of compulsory personal services in any form, whether paid or unpaid, shall be prohibited and punishable by law, except in cases prescribed by law for all citizens.

ARTICLE 12

The peoples concerned shall be safeguarded against the abuse of their rights and shall be able to take legal proceedings, either individually or through their representative bodies, for the effective protection of these rights. Measures shall be taken to ensure that members of these peoples can understand and be understood in legal proceedings, where necessary through the provision of interpretation or by other effective means.

PART II - LAND

ARTICLE 13

1. In applying the provisions of this Part of the Convention governments shall respect the special importance for the

cultures and spiritual values of the peoples concerned of their relationship with the lands or territories, or both as applicable, which they occupy or otherwise use, and in particular the collective aspects of this relationship.

2. The use of the term "lands" in Articles 15 and 16 shall include the concept of territories, which covers the total environment of the areas which the peoples concerned occupy or otherwise use.

ARTICLE 14

1. The rights of ownership and possession of the peoples concerned over the lands which they traditionally occupy shall be recognised. In addition, measures shall be taken in appropriate cases to safeguard the right of the peoples concerned to use lands not exclusively occupied by them, but to which they have traditionally had access for their subsistence and traditional activities. Particular attention shall be paid to the situation of nomadic peoples and shifting cultivators in this respect.
2. Governments shall take steps as necessary to identify the lands which the peoples concerned traditionally occupy, and to guarantee effective protection of their rights of ownership and possession.
3. Adequate procedures shall be established within the national legal system to resolve land claims by the peoples concerned.

ARTICLE 15

1. The rights of the peoples concerned to the natural resources pertaining to their lands shall be specially safeguarded. These rights include the right of these peoples to participate in the use, management and conservation of these resources.
2. In cases in which the State retains the ownership of mineral or sub-surface resources or rights to other resources

pertaining to lands, governments shall establish or maintain procedures through which they shall consult these peoples, with a view to ascertaining whether and to what degree their interests would be prejudiced, before undertaking or permitting any programmes for the exploration or exploitation of such resources pertaining to their lands. The peoples concerned shall wherever possible participate in the benefits of such activities, and shall receive fair compensation for any damages which they may sustain as a result of such activities.

ARTICLE 16

1. Subject to the following paragraphs of this Article, the peoples concerned shall not be removed from the lands which they occupy.
2. Where the relocation of these peoples is considered necessary as an exceptional measure, such relocation shall take place only with their free and informed consent. Where their consent cannot be obtained, such relocation shall take place only following appropriate procedures established by national laws and regulations, including public inquiries where appropriate, which provide the opportunity for effective representation of the peoples concerned.
3. Whenever possible, these peoples shall have the right to return to their traditional lands, as soon as the grounds for relocation cease to exist.
4. When such return is not possible, as determined by agreement or, in the absence o such agreement, through appropriate procedures, these peoples shall be provided in all possible cases with lands of quality and legal status at least equal to that of the lands previously occupied by them, suitable to provide for their present needs and future development. Where the peoples concerned express a preference for compensation in money or in kind, they shall be so compensated under appropriate guarantees.

5. Persons thus relocated shall be fully compensated for any resulting loss or injury.

ARTICLE 17

1. Procedures established by the peoples concerned for the transmission of land rights among members of these peoples shall be respected.
2. The peoples concerned shall be consulted whenever consideration is being given to their capacity to alienate their lands or otherwise transmit their rights outside their own community.
3. Persons not belonging to these peoples shall be prevented from taking advantage of their customs or of lack of understanding of the laws on the part of their members to secure the ownership, possession or use of land belonging to them.

ARTICLE 18

Adequate penalties shall be established by law for unauthorised intrusion upon, or use of, the lands of the peoples concerned, and governments shall take measures to prevent such offences.

ARTICLE 19

National agrarian programmes shall secure to the peoples concerned treatment equivalent to that accorded to other sectors of the population with regard to:

(a) the provision of more land for these peoples when they have not the area necessary for providing the essentials of a normal existence, or for any possible increase in their numbers;

(b) the provision of the means required to promote the development of the lands which these peoples already possess.

PART III - RECRUITMENT AND CONDITIONS OF EMPLOYMENT

ARTICLE 20

1. Governments shall, within the framework of national laws and regulations, and in co-operation with the peoples concerned, adopt special measures to ensure the effective protection with regard to recruitment and conditions of employment of workers belonging to these peoples, to the extent that they are not effectively protected by laws applicable to workers in general.
2. Governments shall do everything possible to prevent any discrimination between workers belonging to the peoples concerned and other workers, in particular as regards:
   (a) admission to employment, including skilled employment, as well as measures for promotion and advancement;
   (b) equal remuneration for work of equal value;
   (c) medical and social assistance, occupational safety and health, all social security benefits and any other occupationally related benefits, and housing;
   (d) the right of association and freedom for all lawful trade union activities, and the right to conclude collective agreements with employers or employers' organisations.
3. The measures taken shall include measures to ensure:
   (a) that workers belonging to the peoples concerned, including seasonal, casual and migrant workers in agricultural and other employment, as well as those employed by labour contractors, enjoy the protection afforded by national law and practice to other such workers in the same sectors, and that they are fully informed of their rights under labour legislation and of the means of redress available to them;

(b) that workers belonging to these peoples are not subjected to working conditions hazardous to their health, in particular through exposure to pesticides or other toxic substances;

(c) that workers belonging to these peoples are not subjected to coercive recruitment systems, including bonded labour and other forms of debt servitude;

(d) that workers belonging to these peoples enjoy equal opportunities and equal treatment in employment for men and women, and protection from sexual harassment.

4. Particular attention shall be paid to the establishment of adequate labour inspection services in areas where workers belonging to the peoples concerned undertake wage employment, in order to ensure compliance with the provisions of this Part of this Convention.

PART IV - VOCATIONAL TRAINING, HANDICRAFTS AND RURAL INDUSTRIES

ARTICLE 21

Members of the peoples concerned shall enjoy opportunities at least equal to those of other citizens in respect of vocational training measures.

ARTICLE 22

1. Measures shall be taken to promote the voluntary participation of members of the peoples concerned in vocational training programmes of general application.

2. Whenever existing programmes of vocational training of general application do not meet the special needs of the peoples concerned, governments shall, with the participation of these peoples, ensure the provision of special training programmes and facilities.

3. Any special training programmes shall be based on the economic environment, social and cultural conditions and

practical needs of the peoples concerned. Any studies made in this connection shall be carried out in co-operation with these peoples, who shall be consulted on the organisation and operation of such programmes. Where feasible, these peoples shall progressively assume responsibility for the organisation and operation of such special training programmes, if they so decide.

ARTICLE 23

1. Handicrafts, rural and community-based industries, and subsistence economy and traditional activities of the peoples concerned, such as hunting, fishing, trapping and gathering, shall be recognised as important factors in the maintenance of their cultures and in their economic self-reliance and development. Governments shall, with the participation of these people and whenever appropriate, ensure that these activities are strengthened and promoted.
2. Upon the request of the peoples concerned, appropriate technical and financial assistance shall be provided wherever possible, taking into account the traditional technologies and cultural characteristics of these peoples, as well as the importance of sustainable and equitable development.

PART V - SOCIAL SECURITY AND HEALTH

ARTICLE 24

Social security schemes shall be extended progressively to cover the peoples concerned, and applied without discrimination against them.

ARTICLE 25

1. Governments shall ensure that adequate health services are made available to the peoples concerned, or shall provide them with resources to allow them to design and deliver such services under their own responsibility and control, so that they may enjoy the highest attainable

standard of physical and mental health.

2. Health services shall, to the extent possible, be community-based. These services shall be planned and administered in co- operation with the peoples concerned and take into account their economic, geographic, social and cultural conditions as well as their traditional preventive care, healing practices and medicines.
3. The health care system shall give preference to the training and employment of local community health workers, and focus on primary health care while maintaining strong links with other levels of health care services.
4. The provision of such health services shall be co-ordinated with other social, economic and cultural measures in the country.

PART VI-EDUCATION AND MEANS OF COMMUNICATION

ARTICLE 26

Measures shall be taken to ensure that members of the peoples concerned have the opportunity to acquire education at all levels on at least an equal footing with the rest of the national community.

ARTICLE 27

1. Education programmes and services for the peoples concerned shall be developed and implemented in co-operation with them to address their special needs, and shall incorporate their histories, their knowledge and technologies, their value systems and their further social, economic and cultural aspirations.
2. The competent authority shall ensure the training of members of these peoples and their involvement in the formulation and implementation of education programmes, with a view to the progressive transfer of responsibility for the conduct of these programmes to these peoples as appropriate.

3. In addition, governments shall recognise the right of these peoples to establish their own educational institutions and facilities, provided that such institutions meet minimum standards established by the competent authority in consultation with these peoples. Appropriate resources shall be provided for this purpose.

ARTICLE 28

1. Children belonging to the peoples concerned shall, wherever practicable, be taught to read and write in their own indigenous language or in the language most commonly used by the group to which they belong. When this is not practicable, the competent authorities shall undertake consultations with these peoples with a view to the adoption of measures to achieve this objective.
2. Adequate measures shall be taken to ensure that these peoples have the opportunity to attain fluency in the national language or in one of the official languages of the country.
3. Measures shall be taken to preserve and promote the development and practice of the indigenous languages of the peoples concerned.

ARTICLE 29

The imparting of general knowledge and skills that will help children belonging to the peoples concerned to participate fully and on an equal footing in their own community and in the national community shall be an aim of education for these peoples.

ARTICLE 30

1. Governments shall adopt measures appropriate to the traditions and cultures of the peoples concerned, to make known to them their rights and duties, especially in regard to labour, economic opportunities, education and health matters, social welfare and their rights deriving from this Convention.

2. If necessary, this shall be done by means of written translations and through the use of mass communications in the languages of these peoples.

ARTICLE 31

Educational measures shall be taken among all sections of the national community, and particularly among those that are in most direct contact with the peoples concerned, with the object of eliminating prejudices that they may harbor in respect of these peoples. To this end, efforts shall be made to ensure that history textbooks and other educational materials provide a fair, accurate and informative portrayal of the societies and cultures of these peoples.

PART VII - CONTACTS AND CO-OPERATION ACROSS BORDERS

ARTICLE 32

Governments shall take appropriate measures, including by means of international agreements, to facilitate contacts and co-operation between indigenous and tribal peoples across borders, including activities in the economic, social, cultural, spiritual and environmental fields

PART VIII - ADMINISTRATION

ARTICLE 33

1. The governmental authority responsible for the matters covered in this Convention shall ensure that agencies or other appropriate mechanisms exist to administer the programmes affecting the peoples concerned, and shall ensure that they have the means necessary for the proper fulfilment of the functions assigned to them.

2. These programmes shall include:

   (a) the planning, co-ordination, execution and evaluation, in co-operation with the peoples concerned, of the measures provided for in this Convention;

(b) the proposing of legislative and other measures to the competent authorities and supervision of the application of the measures taken, in co-operation with the peoples concerned.

PART IX - GENERAL PROVISIONS

ARTICLE 34

The nature and scope of the measures to be taken to give effect to this Convention shall be determined in a flexible manner, having regard to the conditions characteristic of each country.

ARTICLE 35

The application of the provisions of this Convention shall not adversely affect rights and benefits of the peoples concerned pursuant to other Conventions and Recommendations, international instruments, treaties, or national laws, awards, custom or agreements.

PART X- FINAL PROVISIONS

ARTICLE 36

This Convention revises the Indigenous and Tribal Populations Convention, 1957.

ARTICLE 37

The formal ratifications of this Convention shall be communicated to the Director-General of the International Labour Office for registration.

ARTICLE 38

1. This Convention shall be binding only upon those Members of the International Labour Organisation whose ratifications have been registered with the Director-General.
2. It shall come into force twelve months after the date on which the ratifications of two Members have been registered with the Director-General.

3. Thereafter, this Convention shall come into force for any Member twelve months after the date on which its ratification has been registered.

ARTICLE 39

1. A Member which has ratified this Convention may denounce it after the expiration of ten years from the date on which the Convention first comes into force, by an act communicated to the Director-General of the International Labour Office for registration. Such denunciation shall not take effect until one year after the date on which it is registered.
2. Each Member which has ratified this Convention and which does not, within the year following the expiration of the period of ten years mentioned in the preceding paragraph, exercise the right of denunciation provided for in this Article, will be bound for another period of ten years and, thereafter, may denounce this Convention at the expiration of each period of ten years under the terms provided for in this Article.

ARTICLE 40

1. The Director-General of the International Labour Office shall notify all Members of the International Labour Organisation of the registration of all ratifications and denunciations communicated to him by the Members of the Organisation.
2. When notifying the Members of the Organisation of the registration of the second ratification communicated to him, the Director-General shall draw the attention of the Members of the Organisation to the date upon which the Convention will come into force.

ARTICLE 41

The Director-General of the International Labour Office shall communicate to the Secretary-General of the United Nations for registration in accordance with Article 102 of the Charter of the United Nations full particulars of all ratifications and acts of denunciation registered by him in accordance with the provisions of the preceding Articles.

ARTICLE 42

At such times as it may consider necessary the Governing Body of the International Labour Office shall present to the General Conference a report on the working of this Convention and shall examine the desirability of placing on the agenda of the Conference the question of its revision in whole or in part.

ARTICLE 43

1. Should the Conference adopt a new Convention revising this Convention in whole or in part, then, unless the new Convention otherwise provides -
   (a) the ratification by a Member of the new revising Convention shall ipso jure involve the immediate denunciation of this Convention, notwithstanding the provisions of Article 39 above, if and when the new revising Convention shall have come into force;
   (b) as from the date when the new revising Convention comes into force this Convention shall cease to be open to ratification by the Members.
2. This Convention shall in any case remain in force in its actual form and content for those Members which have ratified it but have not ratified the revising Convention.

ARTICLE 44

The English and French versions of the text of this Convention are equally authoritative.

THE ENVIRONMENT (PROTECTION) ACT, 1986 NO. 29 TO 1986 (INDIA)

An Act to provide for the protection and improvement of environment and for matters connected therewith:

WHEREAS the decisions were taken at the United Nations Conference on the Human Environment held at Stockholm June, 1972, in which India participated, to take appropriate steps for the protection and improvement of human environment;

AND WHEREAS it is considered necessary further to implement the decisions aforesaid in so far as they relate to the protection and improvement of environment and the prevention of hazards to human beings, other living creatures, plants and property;

BE it enacted by Parliament in the Thirty-seventh Year of the Republic of India as follows :-

CHAPTER I

PRELIMINARY

1. Short title, extent and commencement

(1) This Act may be called the Environment (Protection) Act, 1986.

(2) It extends to the whole of India.

(3) It shall come into force on such date as the Central Government may, by notification in the Official Gazette, appoint and different dates may be appointed for different provisions of this Act and for different areas.

2. Definitions

In this Act, unless the context otherwise requires-

(a) "environment" includes water, air and land and the inter-relationship which exists among and between water, air and land, and human beings, other living creatures, plants, micro-organism and property;

(b) "environmental pollutant" means any solid, liquid or gaseous substance present in such concentration as may be, or tend to be, injurious to environment;

(c) "environmental pollution" means the presence in the environment of any environmental pollutant;

(d) "handling", in relation to any substance, means the manufacture, processing, treatment, package, storage, transportation, use, collection, destruction, conversion, offering for sale, transfer or the like of such substance;

(e) "hazardous substance" means any substance or preparation which, by reason of its chemical or physico-chemical properties or handling, is liable to cause harm to human beings, other living creatures, plant, micro-organism, property or the environment;

(f) "occupier", in relation to any factory or premises, means a person who has control over the affairs of the factory or the premises and includes in relation to any substance, the person in possession of the substance;

(g) "prescribed" means prescribed by rules made under this Act.

CHAPTER II

GENERAL POWERS OF THE CENTRAL GOVERNMENT

3. Power of Central Government to take measures to protect and improve environment

(1) Subject to the provisions of this Act, the Central Government, shall have the power to take all such measures

as it deems necessary or expedient for the purpose of protecting and improving the quality of the environment and preventing controlling and abating environmental pollution.

(2) In particular, and without prejudice to the generality of the provisions of sub-section (1), such measures may include measures with respect to all or any of the following matters, namely :-

(i) co-ordination of actions by the State Governments, officers and other authorities,-

(a) under this Act, or the rules made thereunder, or

(b) under any other law for the time being in force which is relatable to the objects of this Act;

(ii) planning and execution of a nation-wide programme for the prevention, control and abatement of environmental pollution;

(iii) laying down standards for the quality of environment in its various aspects;

(iv) laying down standards for emission or discharge of environmental pollutants from various sources whatsoever:

Provided that different standards for emission or discharge may be laid down under this clause from different sources having regard to the quality or composition of the emission or discharge of environmental pollutants from such sources;

(v) restriction of areas in which any industries, operations or processes or class of industries, operations or processes shall be carried out or shall not be carried out subject to certain safeguards;

(vi) laying down procedures and safeguards for the prevention of accidents which may cause environmental pollution and remedial measures for such accidents;

(vii) laying down procedures and safeguards for the handling of hazardous substances;

(viii) examination of such manufacturing processes, materials and substances as are likely to cause environmental pollution;

(ix) carrying out and sponsoring investigations and research relating to problems of environmental pollution;

(x) inspection of any premises, plant, equipment, machinery, manufacturing or other processes, materials or substances and giving, by order, of such directions to such authorities, officers or persons as it may consider necessary to take steps for the prevention, control and abatement of environmental pollution;

(xi) establishment or recognition of environmental laboratories and institutes to carry out the functions entrusted to such environmental laboratories and institutes under this Act;

(xii) collection and dissemination of information in respect of matters relating to environmental pollution;

(xiii) preparation of manuals, codes or guides relating to the prevention, control and abatement of environmental pollution;

(xiv) such other matters as the Central Government deems necessary or expedient for the purpose of securing the effective implementation of the provisions of this Act.

(3) The Central Government may, if it considers it necessary or expedient so to do for the purpose of this Act, by order, published in the Official Gazette, constitute an authority or authorities by such name or names as may be specified in the order for the purpose of exercising and performing such of the powers and functions, (including the power to

issue directions under section 5) of the Central Government under this Act and for taking measures with respect to such of the matters referred to in sub-section (2) as may be mentioned in the order and subject to the supervision and control of the Central Government and the provisions of such order, such authority or authorities may exercise the powers or perform the functions or take the measures so mentioned in the order as if such authority or authorities has been empowered by this Act to exercise those powers or perform those functions or take such measures.

4. **Appointment of Officers and their powers and functions**.....

5. **Power to give directions** Notwithstanding anything contained in any other law but subject to the provisions of this Act, the Central Government may, in the exercise of its powers and performance of its functions under this Act, issue directions in writing to any person, officer or any authority and such person, officer or authority shall be bound to comply with such directions

Explanation - For the avoidance of doubts, it is hereby declared that the power to issue directions under this section includes the power to direct-

(a) the closure, prohibition or regulation of any industry, operation or process; or

(b) stoppage or regulation of the supply of electricity or water or any other service.

6. **Rules to regulate environment pollution**

(1) The Central Government may, by notification in the Official Gazette, make rules in respect of all or any of the matters referred to in section 3.

(2) In particular, and without prejudice to the generality of the foregoing power, such rules may provide for all or any of the following matters, namely:-

(a) the standards of quality of air, water or soil for various areas and purposes;

(b) the maximum allowable limits of concentration of various environmental pollutants (including noise) for different areas;

(c) the procedures and safeguards for the handling of hazardous substances;

(d) the prohibition and restrictions on the handling of hazardous substances in different areas;

(e) the prohibition and restriction on the location of industries and the carrying on process and operations in different areas;

(f) the procedures and safeguards for the prevention of accidents which may cause environmental pollution and for providing for remedial measures for such accidents.

CHAPTER III

PREVENTION, CONTROL, AND ABATEMENT OF ENVIRONMENTAL POLLUTION

7. Persons carrying on industry operation, etc, not to allow emission or discharge of environmental pollutants in excess of the standards

No person carrying on any industry, operation or process shall discharge or emit or permit to be discharged or emitted any environmental pollutants in excess of such standards as may be prescribed.

8. Persons handling hazardous substances to comply with procedural safeguards.

No person shall handle or cause to be handled any hazardous substance except in accordance with such procedure and after complying with such safeguards as may be prescribed.

9. Furnishing of information to authorities and agencies in certain cases

(1) Where the discharge of any environmental pollutant in excess of the prescribed standards occurs or is apprehended to occur due to any accident or other unforeseen act or event, the person responsible for such discharge and the person in charge of the place at which such discharge occurs or is apprehended to occur shall be bound to prevent or mitigate the environmental pollution caused as a result of such discharge and shall also forthwith-

(a) intimate the fact of such occurrence or apprehension of such occurrence; and

(b) be bound, if called upon, to render all assistance, to such authorities or agencies as may be prescribed.

(2) On receipt of information with respect to the fact or apprehension of any occurrence of the nature referred to in sub-section (1), whether through intimation under that sub-section or otherwise, the authorities or agencies referred to in sub-section (1) shall, as early as practicable, cause such remedial measures to be taken as are necessary to prevent or mitigate the environmental pollution.

(3) The expenses, if any, incurred by any authority or agency with respect to the remedial measures referred to in sub-section (2), together with interest (at such reasonable rate as the Government may, by order, fix) from the date when a demand for the expenses is made until it is paid, may be recovered by such authority or agency from the person concerned as arrears of land revenue or of public demand.

10. Powers of entry and inspection

(1) Subject to the provisions of this 'section, any person empowered by the Central Government in this behalf shall have a right to enter, at all reasonable times with such assistance as he considers necessary, any place-

(a) for the purpose of performing any of the functions of the Central Government entrusted to him;

(b) for the purpose of determining whether and if so in what manner, any such functions are to be performed or whether any provisions of this Act or the rules made there under or any notice, order, direction or authorisation served, made, given or granted under this Act is being or has been complied with;

(c) for the purpose of examining and testing any equipment, industrial plant, record, register, document or any other material object or for conducting a search of any building in which he has reason to believe that an offence under this Act or the rules made there under has been or is being or is about to be committed and for seizing any such equipment, industrial plant, record, register, document or other material object if he has reason to believe that it may furnish evidence of the commission of an offence punishable under this Act or the rules made there under or that such seizure is necessary to prevent or mitigate environmental pollution.

(2) Every person carrying on any industry, operation or process of handling any hazardous substance shall be bound to render all assistance to the person empowered by the Central Government under sub-section (1) for carrying out the functions under that sub-section and if he fails to do so without any reasonable cause or excuse, he shall be guilty of an offence under this Act.

(3) If any person wilfully delays or obstructs any persons empowered by the Central Government under sub-section (1) in the performance of his functions, he shall be guilty of an offence under this Act.

(4) The provisions of the Code of Criminal Procedure, 1973, or, in relation to the State of Jammu and Kashmir, or an

area in which that Code is not in force, the provisions of any corresponding law in force in that State or area shall, so far as may be, apply to any search or seizures under this section as they apply to any search or seizure made under the authority of a warrant issued under section 94 of the said Code or as the case may be, under the corresponding provision of the said law.

11. Power to take sample and procedure to be followed in connection therewith

(1) The Central Government or any officer empowered by it in this behalf, shall have power to take, for the purpose of analysis, samples of air, water, soil or other substance from any factory, premises or other place in such manner as may be prescribed.

(2) The result of any analysis of a sample taken under sub-section (1) shall not be admissible in evidence in any legal proceeding unless the provisions of sub-sections (3) and (4) are complied with.

(3) Subject to the provisions of sub-section (4), the person taking the sample under sub-section (1) shall –

(a) serve on the occupier or his agent or person in charge of the place, a notice, then and there, in such form as may be prescribed, of his intention to have it so analyzed;

(b) in the presence of the occupier or his agent or person, collect a sample for analysis;

(c) cause the sample to be placed in a container or containers which shall be marked and sealed and shall also be signed both by the person taking the sample and the occupier or his agent or person;

(d) send without delay, the container or the containers to the laboratory established or recognized by the Central Government under section 12.

(4) When a sample is taken for analysis under sub-section (1) and the person taking the sample serves on the occupier or his agent or person, a notice under clause (a) of sub-section (3), then

(a) in a case where the occupier, his agent or person wilfully absents himself, the person taking the sample shall collect the sample for analysis to be placed in a container or containers which shall be marked and sealed and shall also be signed by the person taking the sample, and

(b) in a case where the occupier or his agent or person present at the time of taking the sample refuses to sign the marked and sealed container or containers of the sample as required under clause

(c) of sub-section (3), the marked and sealed container or containers shall be signed by the person taking the samples, and the container or containers shall be sent without delay by the person taking the sample for analysis to the laboratory established or recognised under section 12 and such person shall inform the Government Analyst appointed or recognized under section 13 in writing, about the wilful absence of the occupier or his agent or person, or, as the case-may be, his refusal to sign the container or containers.

12. Environmental laboratories

(1) The Central Government may, by notification in the Official Gazette,-

(a) establish one or more environmental laboratories;

(b) recognise one or more laboratories or institutes as environmental laboratories to carry out the functions entrusted to an environmental laboratory under this Act.

(2) The Central Government may, by notification in the Official Gazette, make rules specifying-

(a) the functions of the environmental laboratory;

(b) the procedure for the submission to the said laboratory of samples of air, water, soil or other substance for analysis or tests, the form of the laboratory report thereon and the fees payable for such report;

(c) such other matters as may be necessary or expedient to enable that laboratory to carry out its functions.

13. Government Analysts

The Central Government may by notification in the Official Gazette, appoint or recognize such persons as it thinks fit and having the prescribed qualifications to be Government Analysts for the purpose of analysis of samples of air, water, soil or other substance sent for analysis to any environmental laboratory established or recognised under sub-section (1) of section 12.

14. Reports of Government Analysts

Any document purporting to be a report signed by a Government analyst may be used as evidence of the facts stated therein in any proceeding under this Act.

15. Penalty for contravention of the provisions of the Act and the rules, orders and directions

(1) Whoever fails to comply with or contravenes any of the provisions of this Act, or the rules made or orders or directions issued there under, shall, in respect of each such failure or contravention, be punishable with imprisonment for a term which may extend to five years with fine which may extend to one lakh rupees, or with both, and in case the failure or contravention continues, with additional fine which may extend to five thousand rupees for every day during which such failure or contravention continues after the conviction for the first such failure or contravention.

(2) If the failure or contravention referred to in sub-section (1) continues beyond a period of one year after the date of conviction, the offender shall be punishable with imprisonment for a term which may extend to seven years.

16. Offences by companies

(1) Where any offence under this Act has been committed by a company, every person who, at the time the offence was committed, was directly in charge of, and was responsible to, the company for the conduct of the business of the company, as well as the company, shall be deemed to be guilty of the offence and shall be liable to be proceeded against and punished accordingly:

Provided that nothing contained in this sub-section shall render any such person liable to any punishment provided in this Act, if he proves that the offence was committed without his knowledge or that he exercised all due diligence to prevent the commission of such offence.

(2) Notwithstanding anything contained in sub-section (1), where an offence under this Act has been committed by a company and it is proved that the offence has been committed with the consent or connivance of, or is attributable to any neglect on the part of, any director, manager, secretary or other officer of the company, such director, manager, secretary or other officer shall also deemed to be guilty of that offence and shall be liable to be proceeded against and punished accordingly.

Explanation - For the purpose of this section –

(a) "company" means any body corporate and includes a firm or other association of individuals;

(b) "director", in relation to a firm, means a partner in the firm.

17. Offences by Government Departments

(1) Where an offence under this Act has been committed by any Department of Government, the Head of the Department shall be deemed to be guilty of the offence and shall be liable to be proceeded against and punished accordingly:

Provided that nothing contained in this section shall render such Head of the Department liable to any punishment if he proves that the offence was committed without his knowledge or that he exercise all due diligence to prevent the commission of such offence.

(2) Notwithstanding anything contained in sub-section (1), where an offence under this Act has been committed by a Department of Government and it is proved that the offence has been committed with the consent or connivance of, or is attributable to any neglect on the part of, any officer, other than the Head of the Department, such officer shall also be deemed to be guilty of that offence and shall be liable to be proceeded against and punished accordingly.

CHAPTER IV

MISCELLANEOUS

18. Protection of action taken in good faith

No suit, prosecution or other legal proceeding shall lie against the Government or any officer or other employee of the Government or any authority constituted under this Act or any member, officer or other employee of such authority in respect of anything which is done or intended to be done in good faith in pursuance of this Act or the rules made or orders or directions issued there under.

19. Cognizance of offences

No court shall take cognizance of any offence under this Act except on a complaint made by-

(a) the Central Government or any authority or officer authorised in this behalf by that Government, or

(b) any person who has given notice of not less than sixty days, in the manner prescribed, of the alleged offence and of his intention to make a complaint, to the Central Government or the authority or officer authorised aforesaid.

20. Information, reports or returns

The Central Government may, in relation to its function under this Act, from time to time, require any person, officer, State Government or authority to furnish to it or any statistics, accounts and other information and such person, officer, State Government or other authority shall be bound to do so.

21. Members, officers and employees of the authority constituted under section 3 to be public servants

All the members of the authority, constituted, if any, in pursuance of any provisions of this Act or the rules made or orders or directions issued there under shall be deemed to be public servants within the meaning of section 21 of the Indian Penal Code (45 of 1860).

22. Bar of Jurisdiction

No civil court shall have jurisdiction to entertain any suit or proceeding in respect of anything done, action taken or order or direction issued by the Central Government or any other authority or officer in pursuance of any power conferred by or in relation to its or his functions under this Act.

23. Powers to delegate ....

24. Effect of other laws

(1) Subject to the provisions of sub-section (2), the provisions of this Act and the rules or orders made therein shall have effect notwithstanding anything inconsistent therewith contained in any enactment other than this Act.

(2) Where any act or omission constitutes an offence punishable under this Act and also under any other Act then the offender found guilty of such offence shall be liable to be punished under the other Act and not under this Act.

25. Power to make rules

(1) The Central Government may, by notification in the

Official Gazette, make rules for carrying out the purposes of this Act.

(2) In particular, and without prejudice to the generality of the foregoing power, such rules may provide for all or any of the following matters, namely-

(a) the standards in excess of which environmental pollutants shall not be discharged or emitted under section 7;

(b) the procedure in accordance with and the safeguards in compliance with which hazardous substances shall be handled or caused to be handled under section 8;

(c) the authorities or agencies to which intimation of the fact of occurrence or apprehension of occurrence of the discharge of any environmental pollutant in excess of the prescribed standards shall be given and to whom all assistance shall be bound to be rendered under sub-section (1) of section 9;

(d) the manner in which samples of air, water, soil or other substance for the purpose of analysis shall be taken under sub-section (1) of section 11;

(e) the form in which notice of intention to have a sample analysed shall be served under clause (a) of sub section (3) of section 11;

(f) the functions of the environmental laboratories, the procedure for the submission to such laboratories of samples of air, water, soil and other substances for analysis or test; the form of laboratory report; the fees payable for such report and other matters to enable such laboratories to carry out their functions under sub section (2) of section 12;

(g) the qualifications of Government Analyst appointed or recognised for the purpose of analysis of samples of air, water, soil or other substances under section 13;

(h) the manner in which notice of the offence and the intention to make a complaint to the Central Government shall be given under clause (b) of section 19;

(i) the authority or officer to whom any reports, returns, statistics accounts and other information shall be furnished under section 20;

(j) any other matter which is required to be, or may be, prescribed.

26. Rules made under this Act to be laid before Parliament

Every rule made under this Act shall be laid, as soon as may be after it is made, before each House of Parliament, while it is in session, for a total period of thirty days which may be comprised in one session or in two or more successive sessions, and if, before the expiry of the immediately following the session or the successive sessions aforesaid, both Houses agree in making any modification in the rule or both Houses agree that the rule should not be made, the rule shall thereafter have effect only in such modified form or be of no effect, as the case may be; so, however, that any such modification or annulment shall be without prejudice to the validity of anything previously done under that rule.

BIBLIOGRAPHY

PRIMARY SOURCES

African Charter on Human and Peoples Rights, adopted June 27, 1981, OAU DOC CAB/LEG/67/3 rev. 5, (1982), entered into force October 21, 1986.

American Convention on Human Rights, O.A.S. Treaty Series No. 36, 1144 U.N.T.S. 123 entered into force July 18, 1978

Centres for Disease Control and Prevention, "Update : Human Plague - India, 1994", Morbidity and Mortality Weekly Report, Vol. 43, No. 41, October 21, 1994.

Constitutent Assembly Debates.

Convention on Rights of Child.

Declaration of the Hague (19879) 29 ILM 1308.

Dietrich Schwela, "Public Health Implication of Urban Air Pollution in Developing Countries : paper presented at the 10th World Clean Air Congress, Erjos, Finland, May 28 - June 2, 1995.

Environment Protection Act 1986.

European Convention for the Protection of Human Rights and Fundamental Freedom, 213 U.N.T.S. 222, entered into force September 3, 1953.

European Human Rights Reports, 1987.

European Human Rights Reports, 1991.

General Assembly Resolution 37/189A, paras 1 and 6.

General Assembly Resolution 2398 (xxii), 3 December 1968.

General Assembly Resolution 45/94, 14 December 1990.

Haluk Ozkaynak et al. Ambient Ozone Exposure and Emergency Hospital Admissions and Emergency Room Visits for

Respiratory Problems in 13 U.S. Cities (American Lung Association, Washington D.C., 1996). http://www.who.int/environmental_information/Air/Guidelines/Introduction.htm [World Health Organization]. http://envfor.nic.in.[Ministry of Environment & Forests, Government of India]. http://envfor.nic.in/cpcb/ [Central Pollution Control Board, New Delhi].

International Bill of Human Rights, United Nations, New York.

National Commission on Urbanization, Report of the National Commission on Urbanization, Vol. II, Govt. of India, New Delhi, 1988.

National Family Health Survey (MCH and Family Planning), Delhi 1993, Population Research Centre, Institute of Economic Growth, Delhi.

Preamble, UN Charter, June 26, 1945, 59 Stat. 1031, T.S. 993, 3 Bevans, 1153 entered into force October 24, 1945.

Proceedings of the National Workshop on Environment Statistics, 12-13 June 1998, Goa, Central Statistical Organisation Department of Statistics, Ministry of Planning and Programme Implementation, Govt. of India, New Delhi.

Report of the WHO Commission on Health and Environment, World Health Organisation, Geneva, 1992.

R. Bertollini et al., Environment and Health 1 : Overview and Main European Issues, WHO Regional Publications, European Series, No. 68 (WHO, Copenhagen, 1996).

Selected Decision of the Human Rights Committee, Vol. 2, UN Publication, October 1982 - April 1998.

The Charter of Economic Rights and Duties of States (GA, Res. 32/xxix).

The State of World Environment, United Nations Environment Programme : Annual Review, 1980.

The UN Declaration on Right to Development 1986.

The World Bank, Urban Policy and Economic Development :

An Agenda for the 1990s (The World Bank, Washington, D.C., 1991).

The World Charter for Nature (GA. Res. 3201-2/S-iv).

United Nations Conference on Environment and Development (A/CONF. 151/126 (Vol. 1) 12 August 1992).

United Nations Conference on Human Environment (UN DOC. A/Conf. 48/14/Rev. 1).

U.N.O., Dept. of Social Affairs : Preliminary Report on the World Social Situation with Reference to Standard of Living, New York, 1952.

United Nations (U.N.) Population Division, World Urbanization Prospects : The 1994 Revision (U.N. New York), 1995.

World Development Indicators 1999, The World Bank, Washington DC, USA.

World Health Organization (WHO), Commission on Health and Environment, Report of the Panel on Urbanization (WHO, Geneva, 1992).

World Development Indicators 1999, The World Bank, Washington D.C., USA.

World Health Organisation, Health aspects of environmental pollution control : planning and implementation of national programmes : Report of WHO Expert Committee, Geneva : WHO, 1974.

World Health Organisation, Environmental pollution control in relation to development : report of WHO expert committee, Geneva : WHO, 1985.

WHO : Constitution of the WHO, Geneva, 1964.

WHO, Health Principles of Housing, WHO, Geneva, 1989.

WHO, Housing - The implications for health, Report of a WHO Consultation, WHO, Geneva, 1987.

World Health Organization, Update and Revision of the Air Quality guidelines for Europe, WHO Regional Office for

Europe, Report No. EUR/ICP/EHAZ 94-05/PB01 (WHO, Copenhagen, 1994).

SECONDARY SOURCES

Books

Agarwal, V.P. et al., *Science Development and Environment*, Society of Bio-Sciences, 1987.

Banerjee, Brojendra Nath, *Environmental Pollution and Bhopal Killings*, Delhi, Gian Publishers, 1987.

Bartelmus, Peter, *Environment and Development*, London, Allen and Unwin, 1986.

Barker Ernest, *Political Thought in England (1848-1914)*.

Bhatt, S., *Environmental pollution and water resources management*, New Delhi, Radiant Publishers, 1986.

Capra Fritjof, *The turning point : scientific society and the rising culture*, London : Frontona, 1984.

Centre for Science and Environment, The State of India's Environment, a citizen's report, New Delhi, 1982.

Centre for Science and Environment, The State of India's Environment 1984-85, the second citizen's report, New Delhi, 1985.

Centre for Science and Environment, The State of India's Environment, Citizen's Fifth Report, New Delhi, 1997

Chapman John W., Rousseau, *Totalitarian or Liberal*, New York, Columbia University Press, 1956.

Chaturvedi, R.G., *State and Rights of Man*, Delhi, Metropolitan Book Co., 1971.

Chhatwal, G.R. and Others, *Encyclopedia of Environmental Pollution and its Control*, Vol. I, New Delhi, Anmol Publications, 1989.

Cobb, Johnm B., Jr., *Sustainability : Economic, Ecology and Justice*, Maryknoll, NY, USA, Orbis Books, 1992.

Culyer, A.J. (ed.), *Economic policies and social goals : aspects of public choice*, London, Martin Robertson, 1974.

Davidson Scott, *Human Rights*, Philadelphia Open University Press, 1993.

Desh Bandhu and Others (ed.), *Environmental Management*, (selected papers at seminar held at Indian National Science Academy during June 5-7, 1980), New Delhi : Indian Environmental Society, 1981.

Desh Bandhu and others, Environment education for conservation and development : Proceedings of the Second International Conference on Environmental Education, New Delhi, Indian Environmental Society, 1987.

Diwan, Paras (ed.), *Environmental protection : problems, policy administration*, New Delhi, Deep and Deep Publishers, 1987.

Diwan Paras (ed.), *Human Rights and Law*, New Delhi, Deep and Deep Publications, 1996.

D'Monte, Darryl, *Temples or tombs ?, Industry versus environment three controversites*, New Delhi, Centre for Science and Environment, 1985.

Dommen, Caroline. *Joining hands for the Future Human Rights and Environment*, peoples for human rights, IMADR Year Book 3, 1991.

Draft Earth Charter, 26 August 1991, H. Hohmann (ed.), Basic Documents of International Environment Law, Vol. 3, 1992.

E. Barker, *The Political Thought of Plato and Aristotle*, New York, Dover Publications, 1959.

Encyclopedia of Britiannica, 15th Edition, Vol. 20, 1985.

Environmental Planning and Coordination Organization, Bhopal National Seminar on Environment : Macro level planning, policies and strategies, Bhopal Feb. 8-10, 1984 Report, Bhopal : The organization, 1984.

Etherington, John R., *Environment and plan ecology*, New Delhi, Wiley Eastern Publishers, 1976.

Feldman David, *Civil liberties and Human Rights in England and Wales*, New York, Oxford University Press, 1993.

George H. Sabine, A History of Political History Delhi, Oxford and JBH Publishing Co., 1961.

Goswami, Deep., A handbook on pollution control by industries and government bodies - with Supreme Court decisions, New Delhi, Emcon Business Review, 1988.

Gwyer and Others, *A Speeches and Documents on the Indian Constitution*, London, Oxford University Press, 1957.

Harrison M. Roy, *Pollution, Causes, Effects and Control*, Royal Society of Chemistry, Cambridge, 2001.

Holgate, M.W., *A Perspective on Environmental Pollution*, London, 1979.

Indian Institute of Public Administration, New Delhi, Environmental Policy in India, edited by Shekhar Singh, New Delhi, The Institute, 1984.

Jain, Suresh and others, *Environmental Laws in India*, Indore : The Lawyers Home, 1984.

Katyal, T. and others, *Environmental Pollution*, New Delhi, Anmol Publishers, 1989.

Kalash Thakur, *Environmental Protection Law and Policy in India*, Deep and Deep Publications, New Delhi, 1997.

Kay, David A. and others, *Environmental protection : The international dimension*, Totowa, Allanheld Publishers, 1983.

Khoshoo, T.N., *Environmental concerns and strategies*, New Delhi : Times Press, 1984.

Kothari, A., *Understanding Biodiversity. Life Sustainability and Equity*, Orient Longman Ltd., 1997.

Krishna Iyer, V.R., *Environmental pollution and law*, Indore : Vedpal Law House, 1984.

Kumar, R. (ed.), *Environmental pollution and health hazards in India*, New Delhi, Ashish Publishers, 1987.

Linda, Starke (ed.), State of the World, 1987 : A worldwatch Institute report on progress toward a sustainable society, New York : W.W. Nortion, 1984.

Lohani, Bindu N., *Environment quality management*, New Delhi : South Asia, 1984.

Mahadevan, Kuttan, *Ecology, Development and Population Problems*, B.R. Publishers, Delhi, 1992.

Malviya, R.A. *Environmental pollution and its control under international law*, Allahabad, Chaugh Publishers, 1987.

Mani, M.S., *Ecology and Evolution*, Satish Book Enterprise, 1983.

Mellanky, Kenneth (ed.), *Air pollution, acid rain and environment*, London : Elsevir Applied Science, n.d. 129 p.

Mohan, I., *Environmental Awareness and urban development*, New Delhi, Ashish Publications, 1988.

Mohan, I., *Environment and habitat, New Delhi*, Ashish Publications, 1989.

Mukund, G.R., *Global Environmental Politics*, Oxford University Press, New Delhi, 1997.

Murphy, Earl Finbar, *Man and his environment : Law*, Harper and Row Publishers, 1971.

N. Rajalakshmi, *Environment and Economic Development*, Manak Publishers, Delhi, 2000.

Paine Thomas, *Rights of Man (1791-92)*, Everyman Ed., 1958.

Pal Chandra, *Environmental pollution and development : Environmental law, policy and role of judiciary*, New Delhi, Mittal Publications, 1999.

Parikh, S. Kirit and Others, *India Development Report 1997*, Delhi, Oxford University Press.

R.A. Malviya, *Environmental Pollution and its Control under International Law*, Allahabad : Chung (1987).

Rama Rao, R., *Environment : problems of developed and developing countries*, New Delhi : Economic and Scientific Research Foundation, 1976.

Ruster, Beand and Others (ed.), *International protection of the environment : treaties and related documents*, New York : Oceana, 1982.

Sapra, R.K. (ed.), *Environment management in India*, New Delhi, Ashish Publications, 1987.

Sharma, R.C., *Environmental Education*, 2nd rev. ed., New Delhi, Metropolitan Book Co., 1986.

Shiva, Vandana, *Staying alive women, ecology and survival in India*, New Delhi : Kali for Women, 1988.

Singh, S.P., *Population Affluence and Ecological Demand, Glimpse of Ecology*, Indian Scientific Publishers, Jaipur, 1978.

Singh, Sukhpal, *Judicial Response to Environmental Pollution in India*, LL.M. Dissertation (unpublished) 1997, 174 p. Law School, B.H.U. Varanasi.

Singh, Ram Bali, *Studies in Environment and development*, New Delhi : Commonwealth, 1988.

Stewart, Charles T., *Air pollution, human health and public policy*, Lexington Books, 1983.

Turner, R. Kerry (ed.), *Sustainable environmental management : principles and practice*, Boulder, Westview Publishers, 1988.

Weeramantry, C.G., *Human Rights and Scientific and Technological Development*, United Nations University Press, 1990.

Weeramantry, C.G., *Impact of Technology on Human Rights, Global Case Studies*, UN University Press, 1990.

World Commission on Environment and Development, Our Common Future, Delhi, Oxford University Press, 1987.

World Environment, 1972-1982, New York : Unipur, 1982.

World Resources Institute, Improving environmental co-operation : The roles of multinational corporations and developing countries, Washington, DC : The Institute, 1984.

ARTICLES

Adler Robert, Reauthorizing the Clean Water Act : Looking to Tangible Values, *Water Resource Bulletin*, Vol. 30, No. 5, 1994.

Alappat, B.J. and Dixit, A.K., Pollution of the space, *Yojana*, 43(2) February 1999.

Arden C. Pope III et al., Particulate Air Pollution as a Predictor of Mortality in a Prospective Study of U.S. Adults, *American Journal of Respiratory and Critical Care Medicine*, Vol. 151, No. 3, 1995.

Bagachi, Samar, Environment problems with special reference to India, *Radical Humanist*, 62(1), April 1998.

Chandra, M., Environmental pollution due to cadmium, mercury lead, arsenic, *School Science*, 35(3), September 1997.

Chattopadhyay, Tapan Kumar, Environment and survival, *Socialist Perspective*, 24(3-4), December 1996 - March 1997.

Dayakrishan and Ganda, I.C., Deteriorating trend in visibility at IGI Airport (Palam) Due to increased load of Air Pollution over Delhi, *Vayu Mandal*, 18(1-2), 1988.

Durrany, K.S., People's response to the environmental problems of Jahanpanah city forest. *Religion and Society*, 37(2), 1990.

Gupta, R.G., Mega cities would be polluted by 2010 A.D. : Case exmaple of Delhi, *Dilli Vikas Varta*, 1(2), 1990.

Hans Nagpaul, The slum and squatter settlements in metropolitan India : review of some strategies for better urban environment, *Indian Journal of Social Research*, Vol. 23, No. 1, 1982

Hardoy Jorge, E., Urban change in the Third World : Are recent trends a useful pointer to the urban future, *Habitat International*, Vol. 10, No. 3, 1986.

Jain, P.C., Environmental pollution : Dangers and remedies. *Kautilya*, 18(12), 1997-98.

Jha, Gangadhar, Land Nationalisation in India : A policy analysis, *Nagarlok*, Vol. 15, No. 2, 1983.

Kapoor, Rajesh, The ugly face of green justice, *Human Scape*, 6(1), 1999.

Khatkar, R.K. and Kundu, P.K. Extent and effect of environment pollution, *Kautilya*, 18(1-2), 1997-98.

Khillare, P.S., Air pollution in Delhi, *JNU News*, 9(5), August 1988.

Loganey, Shalini and Kakkor, Saleena, Environment, *First City*, August 1993.

Muzumdar, Madhushree, EIA, SEA and carrying capacity as tool for urban environmental management, *Urban India*, 16(2), July-December 1996.

Measures taken for fighting pollution in Delhi, *Delhi Garden Magazine* (Flower Show Number 1990), 21(1), 1990.

Order that felled a city, *Economic and Political Weekly*, 32(26), 28 June 1997.

Pandey, Rita, Fiscal options for vehicular pollution control in Delhi, *Economic and Political Weekly*, 33(45), 7 November 1998.

Peter, A. et al., Accute effects of exposure to high levels of air pollution in Eastern Europe. *American Journal of Epidemiology*, Vol. 144, No. 6, 1996.

Raghunandha Reddy, A., Environmental pollution in India : Legal control mechanism, *Indian Socio-Legal Journal*, 23, 1997.

Ray, Aloka, Noise pollution in Calcutta, *Asian Studies*, 16(1), January-June 1998.

Roychowdhury Anumita, Linking Threat, *Down to Earth*, Vol. 6, No. 14, Dec. 15, 1997.

Satterthwante David, The Impact of Health of Urban Environment, *Environment and Urbanization*, Vol. 5, No. 2, 1983.

Saxena, V.K. et al., Earthquake in Maharashtra : Impact Assessment of Communicable Diseases Potential, *Journal of Basic and Applied Medicine*, Vol. 2, No. 1, 1993.

Shaw, Avantika, I., Environmental degradation in an Indian metropolis : The case of social pollution in Lucknow, *Indian National Geographer*, 7(1-2), 1992.

Shukla, Nandita and Pandey, Mahendra, Environmental pollutants and immune system, *Yojana*, 43(2), February 1999.

Sundaram, Sakunthala and Sundaram, Vidya, Environmental impact of air pollution, *Kisan World*, 25(7), July 1998.

Tiwari, D.N., Environmental protection for survival, *Manthan*, 18(3), July-September 1997.

Vigotti, M. et al., Short term effects of urban air pollution respiratory health in Milan Italy, *American Journal of Epidemiology and Community Health*, Vol. 50, 1996.

Journals / periodicals / Magazines

American Journal of Epidemiology (Maryland).

American Journal of Respiratory and Critical Care Medicine (New York).

Asian Studies (Calcutta).

Down to Earth (New Delhi).

Economic and Political Weekly (Mumbai).

Environment and Urbanizaiton (London).

Environmental Health Perspectives (North Carolina USA).

Frontline (Chennai).

Indian Journal of Public Administration (New Delhi).

Indian Journal of Social Research. (Meerut).

Journal of Basic and Applied Medicine.

Journal of Epidemiology and Community Health. (The Nethelands).

Manthan (New Delhi).

Nagarlok (New Delhi).

News Week (New York).

Peoples Democracy (New Delhi).

Social Action (New Delhi).

Stanford Journal of International Law (Stanford, California, USA).

Standford Environmental Law Journal (Stanford, California, USA).

Urban India (New Delhi).

Water Resources Bulletin (Oklahoma).

Yojana (New Delhi).

NEWS PAPERS

- Economic Times (New Delhi).
- Hindustan Times (New Delhi).
- Indian Express (Chandigarh).
- New York Times (New York).
- The Hindu (New Delhi).
- The Sunday Times (New Delhi).
- The Times of India (New Delhi).

INDEX